GOD'S PEN

GOD'S PEN

My Story
from
Guilt *to* Grace *to* Peace

JENNIFER HOERL

Copyright © 2016 Jennifer Hoerl
All rights reserved.

Published in the United States by Jennifer Hoerl
www.jenniferhoerl.com

ISBN 978-0-9974094-0-6 (hardcover)
ISBN 978-0-9974094-1-3 (paperback)
ISBN 978-0-9974094-2-0 (ebook)

Library of Congress Control Number: 2016907715

Portions quoted from *A Course in Miracles* are from the Combined Volume Third Edition, 2007, published by the Foundation for Inner Peace.

Portions quoted from *Peace Pilgrim: Her Life and Work in Her Own Words*, spring 1991 edition, were instrumental in telling my story. In the copyright section of the book is the following gracious permission: "People working for peace, spiritual development and the growth of human awareness throughout the world have our willing permission to reproduce material from this book."

I would like to extend this same permission for all of the material in my book.

Cover Design by Laura Duffy
Book Design by Karen Minster and Astrid Lewis Reedy

Contents

Acknowledgments — *vii*
Introduction — *ix*

Part 1: The Goal

Forgiveness Defined – It's Peace — 1
Desire — 10

Part 2: The Journey Defined

It's Just a Story — 19
My Guilt Story — 20
My Grace Story — 28

Part 3: Forgiveness

It's Not a Story – It's Peace — 113
Not a Conclusion – What's Next — 154

More to Share — *159*
References — *187*
About the Author — *189*

Acknowledgments

I want to thank the Foundation for Inner Peace and the Foundation for *A Course in Miracles*. I also want to thank Friends of Peace Pilgrim.

I am thankful to the **Holy Spirit** for being my friend; taking my fear, guilt, and doubt; guiding me; and bringing other friends, family, and teachers into my life as they were needed in my journey. I am grateful for all of the times and lessons we have all shared.

I am thankful to **Jesus** for being my brother and giving me the grace to find my peace.

I am thankful to **Saint Michael** for showing up when I had some doubts.

I am thankful to **God**, my Father, who never left me.

I would also like to acknowledge Bono, Oprah, Joel Osteen, Elizabeth Gilbert, Iyanla Vanzant, Peace Pilgrim, Amy Torres, and Annette Lantos. All are teachers that I want to thank for showing up in my life. Their messages guided me to my goal of peace and forgiveness, and I hope to honor them by sharing their truths, along with my own, through this book.

Introduction

OK, first let me address the title of my book. I think if you asked anyone who knows me, he or she would say that I am pretty humble, but the title of this book seems a little arrogant, right? Who am I to say I am God's pen (which by the way could be my cute pen I splurged on from Tiffany & Co or mostly a BIC, depending on the day.)

When asked about myself, I provide these usual responses: "I am in finance. I grew up as the middle child in the suburbs of Baltimore. I was raised Catholic," etc. While accurate, these responses never seemed to truly define me, and I felt like something was missing. I felt like those things weren't real.

In my search for authenticity, I realized that the things I tell others are just labels—parts of my individual story—and the labels weren't enough for me. I was so much more, and I wanted everyone to see everything about me, which included my strong faith in God. With this realization, I decided to use my story to find God's role in my life, and in doing so, I found guidance from Him. Because of this guidance, I feel I can claim the title of God's pen, because He is writing this book through me.

I also think I can claim this title for all of us, because we are all God's pen, paintbrush, instrument, piece of chalk, voice, etc. These are just the things we use to tell our stories. While our stories represent our individual journeys, I believe there is one goal that we all share on our individual paths. That goal is forgiveness, which I define as being happy with who we really are, with no regrets from the past and no worries for the future. Forgiveness is true freedom and peace.

While I had a sense of forgiveness inside of me, it wasn't until I started following *A Course in Miracles (ACIM)*—which I will refer to as the *Course* going forward—that I really understood what true forgiveness meant and how it could bring such peace. The Course has been a major influence in my life, and I feel one of the purposes of this book is to relay its message.

Several years ago, a friend and teacher gave me a magnet for my refrigerator with a *Course* quote that says this:

"Beneath your words is written the word of God." *(ACIM 2007, W-12.7)*

When she gave it to me, she asked me to read it out loud, and it has been in my heart ever since. And I now feel compelled to be God's pen.

With this encouragement, I want to share my words, both written through my story and accumulated from other teachers on my path. I believe that they are truths we all share that lead us to our common goal of forgiveness. Our stories keep us separate, but our truths connect us. Jesus said that prayers are answered when two or more are joined in truth, so in sharing my words, I hope to unite us all.

This book project started several years ago when I decided I wanted to electronically record all of my diaries and journals. As I did this, and as I was re-reading my words, I realized universal truths were in my writings. These truths kept building on each other, so I think God had been guiding me all along. I really feel like He gave me the title to this book. He created me, and He is my author. So I turned my story over to Him to write. I am just borrowing His pen to pass along the story, and I hope my book will be used as sort of a consolidated spiritual handbook for you to add to your truths.

At first, I didn't want to share my story, because I thought the goal was the only thing that was really important, and while I still believe that, I realized that the truths that lead to our common purpose are found on the journey. There are common obstacles we all have along the path of life, so by sharing my obstacles and their related guides, I hope forgiveness can be obtained and everyone can find peace and happiness.

When I was very young, I was given a diary. I have had some sort of journal ever since, so I have been writing my entire life. My journal entries include poems, short stories and the many thoughts I have written. They include quotes, observations, insights, and messages I have heard or read from other teachers through various books, songs, movies, and shows. Although I did have to break down the level of detail in my entries so that this book wouldn't be over nine hundred pages long, my entries appear exactly as written. I wanted to be completely open and honest with everyone, including myself. I feel by sharing my journals, I am sharing my soul.

My journal entries are not in any particular order within each section, and they are underlined, italicized and denoted by the following pen symbol:

All of the other teachers and sources I came across and documented have such similar messages to my words that my words seemed to be universal truths, and I thought it would be helpful to detail what has guided my path. I want to give those teachers the credit they deserve. They have led the way, so this is also my compilation of what I learned from them to share with you.

I am so thankful to those teachers I encountered, and since I have received, I want to give back. I have always wanted to share their messages with friends and family. However, in the past when I mentioned that I listened to U2, watched Oprah, or read a certain book, others may or may not have been receptive at the time. It was sometimes difficult to bring up advice that may have been helpful, and I wasn't always able to share a particular message. This is why I think God is directing me to share these messages now as divine connections for all.

PART 1
THE GOAL

Chapter 1

Forgiveness Defined – It's Peace

I thought I would start with the goal as a means to introduce the *Course*, and I think it will make it easier to follow my story and understand the lessons I learned.

I believe in a higher power that I call God—other names for this power are Awakened, Consciousness, or Universe. For consistency, I will use God throughout the book. I have also followed Jesus my entire life, and the *Course* was a natural progression in my faith and only expanded my understanding of all of my beliefs.

The *Course* was and has been a huge influence for me. I can't remember when or how it came into my life, but it was definitely through grace. It was a difficult concept for me to grasp at first, so I wasn't consistent in my reading. Then one day it clicked, and I couldn't put it down. I had to see where it led.

The *Course* is a holy book that uses modern education techniques. The *Course* has three components: a text, a workbook for students, and a manual for teachers.

I was fortunate enough to find an incredible mentor not long after I started wholeheartedly doing the *Course*. I met Annette Lantos through a friend, and she had been practicing the *Course* for many years. She is the widow of Congressman Tom Lantos, and they both survived the Holocaust in Nazi-occupied Hungary. She is an amazing person, friend, and teacher, so learning about forgiveness from her was an amazing experience. I can never thank her enough for the lessons she taught me.

A *Course in Miracles* might seem like a strange title, so let me explain. A miracle isn't a divine intervention in the physical world, but a divine intervention in our minds, which heals our thoughts. It is in our minds where true healing begins, so the key to healing our human issues is within our grasp, within our own hearts and minds. In the choice to forgive, we can escape all the pain and suffering of the world. We can bring healing to the hearts of others and we can be reunited with God. That sounds like peace and freedom to me!

The *Course* provides fifty principles of miracles. I have listed some below. *(ACIM 2007, T-1.I)*

Principle 3: "Miracles occur naturally as expressions of love. The real miracle is the love that inspires them. In this sense, everything that comes from love is a miracle."

The Goal

Principle 12: "Miracles are thoughts. Thoughts can represent the lower or bodily level of experience, or the higher or spiritual level of experience. One makes the physical, and the other creates the spiritual."

Principle 13: "Miracles undo the past in the present, and thus release the future."

Principle 14: "Miracles bear witness to truth."

Principle 18: "A miracle is a service. It is the maximal service you can render to another. It is a way of loving your neighbor as yourself. You recognize your own and your neighbor's worth simultaneously."

Principle 20: "Miracles reawaken the awareness that the spirit, not the body, is the altar of truth. This is the recognition that leads to the healing power of the miracle."

Principle 21: "Miracles are natural signs of forgiveness. Through miracles, you accept God's forgiveness by extending it to others."

Principle 26: "Miracles represent freedom from fear. 'Atoning' means 'undoing.' The undoing of fear is an essential part of the atonement value of miracles."

Principle 27: "A miracle is a universal blessing from God through me to all my brothers. It is the privilege of the forgiven to forgive."

Principle 40: "The miracle acknowledges everyone as your brother and mine. It is a way of perceiving the universal mark of God."

So, the miracle is forgiveness, and forgiveness is our common goal. For me, it is the peace, happiness, and unconditional love that I can have now. It is derived from seeing everything, every situation, and everyone, including myself, as if for the first time every time without seeing the story or the drama. It is about accepting what is going on as it is in the current moment. It is remembering happiness from the past, being happy in the present and looking forward to more happiness in the future. It is definitely what I want, because it brings a freedom from guilt, suffering, fear, and from the past. It is peace, love, light, happiness, and home. I believe we are all united in this desire for peace, and we all want these things in our life. If I want peace for myself and others, and if I offer it to myself and others, wouldn't the world be so much better?

The *Course* also says—and I agree—that forgiveness is the only way back to God. Forgiveness undoes our story so that we can move forward with faith.

The Goal

Originally, I was writing this book for my friends, to share with them and tell them all of my truths and the things that they may not know about me—a confession that I hoped would be helpful to them. As a confession though, writing became even more beneficial for me. While in the Bahamas, I took a cab and talked to the driver about my project, and in that short drive, his judgment of my book was that it was a "self-purge." I thought this was a good observation, because while I believe in and aspire to my higher Self every day, I live with my worldly self, which the *Course* often refers to as the body, and it includes the ego, physical body, and emotions. It is an unconscious dream world created by us. The body needs to be corrected through forgiveness, so by writing this book and sharing my story, I am undoing the story of my ego and heading home to peace and happiness. The *Course* uses the lowercased *self* when referring to the body. The uppercased *Self* is used when referring to the spiritual, enlightened, and awakened self - it is the Holy Spirit that God gave us to guide us home.

Below is my interpretation of the Course's premise.

The Goal

1—We are one with God and the Holy Spirit.

2—We had what the *Course* calls "a tiny mad idea" to separate from God. We should have laughed at this idea and returned to God, but instead, we **thought** we left Him.

3—Because we thought we left, we became guilty and afraid that God would punish us. So we took that guilt and fear, and **we** created a second world of an ego self, which is just a dream world where we believe in sin and guilt and are never satisfied or happy. It's our story. We want to go home—to wake up—but we have so much guilt and fear that we don't know how to get back. The *Course* notes this:

> "Yet the Bible says that a deep sleep fell upon Adam, and nowhere is there reference to his waking up. The world has not yet experienced any comprehensive reawaking or rebirth. Such a rebirth is impossible as long as you continue to project or miscreate. It still remains within you, however, to extend as God extended his Spirit to you. In reality this is your only choice, because your free will was given you for your joy in creating the perfect." (*ACIM* 2007, T-2.I.3)

So the good news is that we never left God. We just *think* that we left Him, so we can return to His peace at any moment. God is just waiting for us to decide to wake up from our dream. He doesn't bring any suffering or know anything of it. He only knows love, which is within us as the Holy Spirit—who is the gift God gave us to help us get back to love. I once heard, I can't change the world, but I can change the world in me. How freeing is that? The choice is ours, so we can live in fear and guilt. Or we can choose love and return to God's peace.

Following this premise, the Course says that there is one problem and that there is one solution to *anything* that doesn't give us peace or return us to God. The problem—as stated above—is that we think we have sinned and that we are separate from God. The solution is there is no sin, because we are not truly separate from God. He never left us. When we thought we separated from Him, He gave us the Holy Spirit and Jesus to guide us back to Him. They are using the dream we have created here on earth to undo our fears and erase our stories. If we can undo our fears, we will have more clarity of our higher Self and decide to go home to peace. We are only mistaken in the dream, so we just need to give our stories to the Holy Spirit, be patient, and let things happen as they will, knowing that all will be all right and that anything is possible with God's love. This is giving Him our darkness, so He can remove it and give us the light and clarity we need.

Here's an illustration of how this looks for me:

By undoing my story, I am undoing my dream and returning to God's love and peace.

Through my Catholic upbringing, I knew about the Holy Spirit. It was called the Holy Ghost, and I have to say I really didn't understand when or how it was helping me, but in forgiveness, the Holy Spirit became a true friend. I was always talking to Him—asking for help and ranting about my doubts and fears—and I realized He was using every situation to help me undo my story. All I had to do was go along for the ride and know that He wasn't judging me, that He loved me unconditionally, and that He used everything I experienced as a guide home to peace. I loved having this relationship with Him, so I tried to be that kind of a friend to everyone I met, and it always brought me peace. So my goal was peace for everyone, including myself, and I was ready to give my story to the Holy Spirit to use for all of the peace I desired.

Chapter 2

Desire

Now that the goal is understood, I will begin to explain how it was obtained for me. My guilt story is where I will share most of my worldly journey, which is when I was unconscious of the dream world I was creating – the body, ego, my little self. I felt something wasn't right, and I was looking for external answers to solve my problems.

While living externally, I always had this feeling that something deep and internal was missing from my life. I always wanted more. There was a desire for something I couldn't put my finger on. I wrote everything in my journal, and this yearning is reflected in some of my early poems and short stories below. They demonstrate the confusion, obstacles, and questions I encountered in the past as well as my desire to escape my present situations. While my words and ideas may be different, I think the thoughts behind these ideas are similar for us all. So I have decided to share my thoughts before beginning my story through guilt.

Australia

A new world, a new start.
It may not be better, but it is definitely different.
I need this type of change.

It may seem far or drastic,
But it is a dream that
I don't want to let go.
With every day, it gets closer.

My only fear is that I won't make it,
Not of disappointment.
I can't be disappointed in the grasping
of a dream.

Australia is a dream soon to become reality.

Why Do I Do What I Always Do?

What makes me say the wrong things and act in
the wrong manner? What makes people think
I am different, weird, or strange?
I wish someone and everyone could see the real me.
The person I am inside that never seems to come out right,
that comes out weird or strange.

I wish I could be me and be accepted by others at the
same time.

Haiku
Walking on the path,
Unaware of anything
But him there with me.

I didn't know who the "him" was at the time—I thought "he" was a guy, but now I know "he" was Jesus or the Holy Spirit. Grace was starting.

Love's Path
I sat along the shore, gazing out at the stars and sea, clearing my thoughts, and preparing myself for the future. All at once, I glanced down the coastline and saw him approach. He seemed familiar—not a person from my past but a part of my future.

He came closer, and I felt a certain security and friendship. But there was more.

I began to feel an uncertainty as he passed me. I had a choice to make. I could remain where I was with this uncertainty he had given to my future, leaving me to always wonder if he was the one I was to follow.

My other choice was to follow him and see where he led me. With this choice came more uncertainty and more questions I could not answer. How long would the journey be? And would there be happiness for me at the end?

The Goal

*When I thought further, I thought that perhaps once I began
this journey, I could turn back. But I realized that in
life there is no turning back. I must always move forward.*

*With all these choices, I listened to the beating inside of
me. It was my heart. My heart told me to follow him,
and so I did.*

*For most of the trip, I walked behind. At times, however,
I walked beside him, and we were close—
mostly as friends. It hurt when I left his side,
but hope accompanied me as I walked behind.*

*After what seemed quite a distance travelled, I noticed
something. Along the path I travelled were other paths
that went away from the one I was on. Looking further
down some of these paths, I could see that they led
back to my path. I realized these paths only filled the time
when I was made to follow. They lessened the pain.*

*I began to wonder if all these branches on my path led me
back to him.*

*Perhaps there will be one that will take me on another long
journey with someone else to follow instead of him.*

*No matter whom I follow, however, I will always love him
for beginning my journey, and I will never forget all
he taught me on this journey while I both followed and
walked beside him.*

(This could have been about a guy. I thought I wanted a relationship, but now I know this person was Jesus.)

Two People

Every morning when I look into the mirror, I see two people.
One is who everyone expects me to be.
I am happy to see that person but mainly because others are happy to see him.
He is who I should be, and he is moving in the direction I should be moving.
He is interested in the challenge but needs to be motivated.

The other person is difficult to see.
He is much deeper.
He is not interested in routine and rarely finds satisfaction in small achievements.
He needs excitement and adventure.
He can be caring, warm, and sensitive.
He is not so easy to understand,
So I never give him the credit he often deserves.

Both people, however, are important and special.
Neither should be hidden from the other.
When separated, they can create fear and confusion, but together, they can accomplish anything.

(I wrote this for the guy I was seeing at the time, but it was really about me.)

Untitled

Artistic but not an artist.
Organized and dependable but not in business.
Friendly but not a friend.
In love but not a lover.
Mature but not a woman.

Who am I?
My life is between what I am and what I want to be.
When do I cross over—to happiness?

Undefined

My life—everything about it—is undefined.
My job.
My beliefs.
My family.
My relationships
With friends.
I am so tired of knowing and then not knowing what I want.
I need to obtain at least one goal in my life.
I want to be happy.

Guilt

I hate this feeling.
It stops me from getting what I want.
I always want attention and people to do for me, but when they do, I feel guilty. Why?

Do I not deserve it?
Maybe I really don't want it. But I do!
Why do I feel guilty or awkward every time someone goes out of the way—even in the smallest way—for me?
Maybe that's another way to get attention.
I wish I knew something else I need to try to understand to be happy!

Untitled

Well, here I am about halfway through this journal.
Have I grown?
Have I learned anything about myself, my emotions, my fears, my goals, my dreams, my friends, or my life in general?
I hope that the answers to these questions are yes.
I don't know if at this point in my life, I could honestly answer these questions. Maybe I can by the end of this journal or the next journal or maybe never. But I will always try.

The Struggle

Inside, it twists and turns,
Always creating conflict.
It is unknown
Yet so strong.
At times, it is mild,
But it always leaves a pain.

This confusion never subsides.
It has remained as far as memory serves.
Will it ever flee?
And let me live?

Love to Me

It is a feeling—no strings attached, no obligations,
no responsibilities, and no commitments. Just a feeling
inside that helps you to do or be anything you want.

Unfortunately, it is not always a mutual feeling,
which is why it can bring confusion, sadness, and
despair if it is held on to unrealistically.

The answer is to let go—but how?

Untitled

I don't know what I am feeling anymore.
I don't know why I am feeling what I am.
I don't know what to do to change.
I want to be happy, but I don't know how.
I need to talk to someone, but I don't know who.

What? Why? How? Who? Over and over again in my head!

PART 2

THE JOURNEY DEFINED

Chapter 3

It's Just a Story

At an event in Washington, DC, Oprah had Elizabeth Gilbert—an important teacher for me—speak. Elizabeth Gilbert discussed Joseph Campbell's hero's journey. He says it is a call to adventure that is initially denied until a teacher is met. On this journey, setbacks are encountered but a goal is obtained. Then the hero becomes the teacher. This journey is true for each of us, and using this formula, my journey looks like the following:

- Call to adventure – a deep desire for something more
- Setbacks – denial, guilt and fear that created a story and obstacles
- The goal – forgiveness and peace is found through grace
- Then my teacher role is obtained by passing lessons along in this book!

So the journey is just the story we show the world, and mine can be summed up in these three steps: guilt (living externally) through grace (seeking internally) to forgiveness and peace (living eternally).

CHAPTER 4

My Guilt Story

Before I begin, I want to say that I have had a pretty good life and have experienced a great deal of happiness. While I have had some challenges, my life has been blessed and just keeps getting better and better.

I started out in public school for kindergarten and first grade, and then I attended a Catholic school for second grade through eighth grade. I remember going to church and learning about Jesus's sacrifice for my shame. There is a sacrament called "penance." You had to sit with a priest and confess your sins. I didn't think I had done anything wrong and would have to come up with something. I usually mentioned being disrespectful of my parents, even though that rarely happened. I was mad at them sometimes, so I thought I could use that as a sin. Talk about Catholic guilt—I was creating sins that never occurred and feeling I needed to repent for every bad thought I had. I was letting the outside world tell me I was bad or had done something wrong. I was so young—what sins could I have had? I didn't get it, and I had no idea of how to apply it to my life. I could never be as good as Jesus, and I certainly couldn't die on a cross and suffer the brutality He suffered to get to heaven. What hope was there for me?

We mostly covered the Old Testament in church and school, so I usually only saw the suffering that was necessary to achieve freedom. I watched the Ten Commandments every year and thought we had to go through plagues, hardships, and death to reach a promised land in forty years. Yikes!

During that period of my life, I felt guilty and judged all of the time. It just didn't feel right. I couldn't let go of the shame I had developed. I tried to follow all of the rules—going to church on Sunday, getting good grades, and obeying my parents and elders. I was a good person that never felt good enough, and I was being told I was a sinner.

I took all of my grade-school lessons to a public high school in the city, thinking I would leave the guilt behind me. Then I encountered not feeling adequate enough and peer pressure. I never had the right clothes or enough money for the things I needed—or wanted—to be like everyone else.

I was from a middle-class family, and I grew up in the suburbs of a large city. I had everything I needed growing up. I just didn't realize it at the time. This is the beginning of my worldly, external journey of always wanting more and never feeling satisfied, no matter how much I achieved.

Not knowing what I really wanted to do with my life, I attended a community college. All I knew was that I wanted to make a lot of money, so that I could have everything I thought I wanted—nice clothes, cars, and trips to as many places as possible.

I had many friends and hung out with several guys, until I met someone that I thought I loved. It seemed like he was just like me and wanted all the same things I wanted, so we shopped—a lot! This is when my debt and the constant worry that I would never pay it off started. I also worried that I would never have everything that I wanted. I went from working at Pizza Shack, where I was paid in cash, to Payless ShoeSource to Price Club, where I spent ten years because I was paid well. I was able to keep my debt at a manageable level, while I took trips and went to school, even though I was not sure of what I wanted to do. Although I was having fun, I was struggling internally. I was never really satisfied and was wondering why I wasn't satisfied. I thought I was pursuing all of my dreams—funny! (*Funny* is a word I use often because I see how appropriately it describes my past life. I just laugh now, because my previous, worldly life really is just funny.)

So I knew this guy wasn't right for me. All the signs were there, but I kept telling myself that I loved him and our life together and that he would change into what I needed. I knew these things were not true. But he made me feel like I was living my dream, even though I didn't know what my dream actually was. I really had no clue. I always felt like I wanted more, but

I never knew what "more" meant. I always thought I was missing something, but I never stopped long enough to ask myself what that something was. I was always going to the next thing—a party with friends or the mall. I kept spending money I didn't have and taking trips to places I couldn't afford, thinking these things would fulfill me.

After several years, I finally had a degree in business management with an emphasis in accounting, so it was time for a real career—one with fancy titles, a good salary, and some credibility. I ended up leaving Price Club and got a "real" job with the National Science Foundation as an auditor for the Office of the Inspector General. That sounds impressive, doesn't it? From there, I made a lateral move to the National Credit Union Administration and became an examiner. I was pretty good at it, so one of the credit unions I examined asked me to be their controller, which was a better title that soon led to me becoming a CFO. Wow, my friends seemed impressed. I played it down, but I was kind of impressed too.

Soon after getting the job with the credit union, I parted ways with the guy I thought I loved and became the independent person I knew I could be. Life was good. I bought my own house, had no debt, and thought I would be happy for the rest of my life. I was wrong! I still wasn't satisfied and didn't really know why. I was definitely on a course to something, and I was starting to see God as part of that course.

I determined that I was never really satisfied because I was afraid. I didn't know what I was afraid of at the time, but I knew something wasn't right. I now know that my spiritual, internal desire that I was writing about in my journal often manifested into worldly obstacles that kept me from feeling free, because they were weighing on my soul.

In general, my biggest obstacle was anxiety, or a lack of self-confidence. I had feelings of not being enough and not having enough. I thought that something was missing or could be better. I always worried about what others thought of me. I would feel lazy if I wasn't doing enough or bad if I didn't follow society's expectations. I felt selfish if I wasn't doing enough for others.

I think these feelings are common among us all. I want to share how they showed up for me in my phase of guilt, how I explored them through grace, and—most importantly—how I overcame them through forgiveness. Through each step, these feelings decreased, and then they disappeared almost entirely.

Lack of Money

I have always thought that I needed money and things to make me feel important and to have people accept me, but it seemed there was never enough money to accomplish my goals. This is why when I left home, I had no savings and why I would shop often for instant gratification. I accumulated debt by buying things that

I didn't need and going places that were well outside of my budget. Because I didn't want anyone to know about my debt, I also always felt like I had a secret. I wanted everyone to think I was financially strong.

I always felt like I had to work hard to support my lifestyle, so the good news is that I created a great work ethic. I have always been a valued employee that is respected. The bad news is that I never gave myself credit. I was always afraid that I might lose my job, because I didn't feel good enough.

Physical Body

When I was thirteen, I had a heart murmur that was corrected with open-heart surgery, so health issues have been present through most of my life and have always created some type of fear or anxiety.

With regard to death, I remember hearing someone say that when it was your time to go, God would take you.

I also said the following prayer every night when I was young:

"Now I lay me down to sleep. I pray thee Lord my soul to keep. If I die before I wake, I pray thee Lord my soul to take."

I knew what the prayer meant, but I would fall asleep each night scared that I would not wake up in the morning.

I was also a fan of Billy Joel, and I loved the song "Only the Good Die Young." It spoke to my Catholic ways, but it also scared me, because I thought I was a pretty good person, so I wondered if that meant that I would die soon. Also, Billy Joel said death came down to fate, so for me, either God or something else out of my control would decide whether I lived or died.

So, like everyone, I feared death.

Judgment

I always thought my life should be what everybody else thought it should be, so I always worried about what others thought of me. And in my mind, I was never good enough. I always worried about making a mistake, which is funny, because in my early career, I was always some form of an auditor. I was always looking for others' mistakes, and I worried that I would make a mistake. Again, this fear created a great work ethic and made me thorough and good at my job, but it made me a nervous wreck.

Even when people seemed to compliment me for any wealth or success I obtained, I felt judged and awkward. When I would mention that something good had happened in my life, I would often hear this phrase: "It must be nice." It made me feel judged when people said that because it felt like they thought I had more than them. They thought I was lucky or had some advantage. I was not able to explain that my faith had given me everything I had and that faith was all they needed in their lives. I felt bad for being blessed—which is crazy, right?

I realized that all of my feelings of lack created my judgments of myself and that I was projecting what I thought about myself on others. I was judging them also, and I didn't like this feeling, so I never had total peace.

In my guilt, I was happy on the surface. I was traveling and shopping, accumulating things and proving to the world and myself that my life was perfect. I was always trying to do the right thing, make people like me, and be a good person. I actually was a good person. I just didn't believe that about myself. I didn't understand why, and I became resentful. I was anxious or afraid of something. So I asked myself this: "What am I afraid of?"

In my guilt, I knew about God, but I didn't think He would love me until I was perfect. I thought my answers to my guilt were coming from the outside, and I thought I wasn't being heard. Then I found grace and realized that I needed to go where God would hear me—which was inside. I wanted to eliminate fear and find love.

Chapter 5

My Grace Story

Then Came Grace! Take a Breath!
Actually, grace had been there all along. As I mentioned, my friends thought I was lucky, because I seemed to have such a great life. I also thought I had a great life, but I still wasn't satisfied. I still wanted more, but I couldn't figure out what my real desire was inside.

Through grace, I learned that the yearning inside was my faith—my desire and my willingness to want and expect more rather than settle for what I already had, or even worse, expect bad things to happen. My friends thought I was lucky, but the truth was that I wanted to be happy. I didn't want fear in my life. I was always looking for peace in everything, and that's what I tried to find. I chose the desire for love and happiness over fear.

While I felt guilty, life sometimes seemed difficult, but I had a lot of moments where I knew things would be fine. Those were the moments that I knew God was leading me on a course. The whole time I knew certain truths. I could feel something pulling me in the

The Journey Defined

right direction, but I was frustrated because I didn't know what was pulling me. Looking back at my journals made me realize God was with me all along.

Through grace, I found my path, and many messages presented themselves. These messages are included in some of the following notes I recorded in my journal.

I need to believe that "there is always a better way" and expect it!

"I believe in the sun, even though it doesn't shine.

I believe in love, even when it isn't shown.

I believe in God, even when He doesn't speak." from a wall of a concentration camp in Night, by Elie Wiesel

Faith is a conviction that He can and a hope that He will.

The cry of the soul. The primal cry of separation. The heart's longing for God.

Longing is the greatest gift because it does not allow us to forget Him.

"And all my sorrows end in Your embrace, which You have promised to Your Son, who thought mistakenly that he had wondered from the sure protection of Your loving Arms." (ACIM, W-317.2)

God, Jesus, and the Holy Spirit, help me to feel my Father's embrace, to know I am still in His loving arms with no worries or fears—only love!

I have the same place in God's heart as Jesus. We are the same, so I can accept my Father's love and forgiveness and give love and forgiveness to everyone as Jesus has. Thank

You, God, for this amazing gift.

Now I will guide myself no more. My freedom is found in accepting a new guide. It is found in letting go of my independent goals and accepting the one goal we share together.

Through my journey to this point, I accepted that I had experienced the following things:

- Low self-esteem
- Never being good enough
- Not receiving the respect I deserved
- Wanting to buy love and friendship
- Not being able to say no
- Not being able to get angry
- Feeling shame

I believed in God, but in guilt, I thought He was judging me for these things. In grace, I realized that there was unconditional love and that there was nothing wrong with me. I didn't know that everything was pulling me toward Him, and now, looking back, it seems like everything was aligning to get me to where I am today.

An example of this alignment showed up in my career. I wasn't feeling content with my job at the credit union. I felt like I should be doing something more meaningful, but I didn't know what that really meant either. I decided to leave the credit union and look for a job with a nonprofit organization, thinking that would make me feel more fulfilled. I turned in my notice, and although I was nervous about not having another job at the time, I knew it would all work out somehow. I had always been a U2 fan—which will have its own section below—and I found Bono's organization, DATA, which is now the ONE Campaign, needed a director of finance, so I applied. It took a while, but I got the job. I remember being in Hawaii for the final U2 show on the *Vertigo* tour and seeing the title "DATA" in the back of a book I was reading, and I just knew the job was mine. That was in December, and I started at DATA in May. I knew something was working to lead me there.

Fortunately, while I was going through my season of guilt, seeds were planted to move me through this stage. It was like my yearning caused me to crave a connection with God. I filled this desire with the Bible, church, Bono, Oprah, the Course and other teachers, and I was feeling pretty good—like I was on a path to something. I felt very content but also that there was more. I kept moving and looking for what that "more" was.

I wanted to find true universal love, and I knew it was in me. I figured out that's where I needed to start, so I took what I had learned so far, added a self-help path, and began using the external world for an internal assessment with God. With His grace, I started figuring out that there wasn't too much wrong with me because I was loved unconditionally. Reading John 3:16 proved this. It said: "For God so loved the world that he gave his only begotten Son, that whosoever believed in him should not perish, but have everlasting life."

Jesus took away my shame through His grace, but I needed to keep working internally to bring His grace into my daily life. I wanted to be happy all of the time. Sometimes, we forget just how amazing it is that God cared enough about us to send His only Son to live on earth with us. But He did! And that's really something to celebrate, which I did with more exploration by starting to ask "what?" more instead of "why?"

In an article in a magazine, I was asked this: "What do I want?" Here's how I responded at the time.

What a tough question—I want unconditional love, but I don't know if I can give it. I want to be able to give it. That would make me feel like I was accepted, no matter what. Then I wouldn't have to worry about my flaws. I could breath and be happy with who I am all of the time. I have to love myself, which I think I have started to do. I have good days and bad days. I have to remember that when I am jealous of something or someone, it is because I believe there is a lack in my life, but there is really abundance. There is enough love for everyone, including myself.

I have always been a good listener, friend, and a kind person. If I get nervous around others because I don't know what to say, I shouldn't worry but just be myself and listen. If it was meant to be, it will be, and I shouldn't worry. If it takes so much effort that just means it wasn't meant to be.

I need to have faith that I am here for a reason and that God has a plan that I should put my faith in. I need to not worry about anything or anyone's opinion. I have to be true to myself and do whatever it takes to do this.

I have to realize I am strong and kind. I don't feel kind, because I feel I do nice things to get something for myself—usually attention. I do for others so that they will do for me, but then I am always disappointed or hurt when they don't do for me. Maybe I need to do for myself so that I am not let down. The trouble is I don't always want to do for myself. I want help from others and to be loved. Why do I feel like I don't deserve these things? Why do I turn down help or push people away?

I will be stronger if I accept help, admit my fears, and be honest with others and myself. God, help me to live this new truth and appreciate all that I have, all that I have done, and all that others have helped me with.

I was also asked these questions: "What does being myself look like? What would I say if I were myself?"

I feel like I am an actor—doing, saying, and being what I think is expected of me and what I think others want.

I shut people out when I disagree with how they think but then think of myself as kind. Am I? Or am I the horrible person that some see me as?

I often feel uncomfortable around others. Why? It's like they're going to figure me out, but I don't know what's going on myself.

I want clarity. I want to know how I feel, why I feel what I do, and how to respond with authenticity.

Help me to reach this goal. I feel lost so often.

I think I know right from wrong. Give me the courage and strength to live what is right.

God, please protect my boys. I love them so much. They bring me such joy, warmth, and comfort. Neville's purr when he is content and Phillip's kneading paw when he is happy. Help me to remember their love always and to have it be enough. I want to be happy with all of the blessings I have, especially my two boys. I don't want to need anything else or to never be satisfied. I have so much. I don't want to always feel like I need more or that there is something missing.

The only thing I have to do is love myself and trust God to show me the way. If that is my end result, I should be able to do and say anything without worrying.

I only need to learn from my mistakes, not regret them!

From these questions, I realized I was feeling confused and wanted answers, so I started talking to God more and turning things over to Him more.

This is where the real work began, and I had many teachers along the way. They provided valuable lessons, so in an effort to share their truths in these lessons, I will provide more detail about the teachers and their quotes and comments in this section.

Lessons Put on My Path in Early Years

I took a stress-management class in college, and it was the best class I ever attended. I wish I could remember my teacher's name because his lessons followed me throughout my life, and I have been blessed by hearing them at such an early stage. Sometimes I used them only as lip service, and I may not have actually always believed them, but I know sometimes we have to "fake it" to "make it." Those lessons became constant reminders to see things differently.

Accountability

One of the most significant messages I received was that people and things don't upset me. Instead I *let* people and things upset me. This was a huge revelation for me for two reasons. Firstly, it brought the issue inside where I could deal with it internally with my higher Self and where I know it could be corrected. Secondly, it gave *me* control over every situation, because I was accountable for what I was thinking. Now, as inspiring as that sounds, I didn't always use this revelation well and would blame the world for my problems—and I still do sometimes—but it was a good building block. The more I used it, the more I remembered its strength, and I can truly say that much less bothers me these days, because I don't let things bother me so much!

BAD

The next lesson I learned in this class played on an acronym for the word *bad*. Often we look back in regret at some of the "bad" decisions that we made. We go over and over in our heads what we should have, could have, or would have done. We spend so much time reflecting that we don't look to the future. Then we lose hope. If in those moments, we would just stop and think of "BAD," as an acronym to stand for "Best Available Data," because that is what we used at the time to make the decision, then forgive ourselves for making a mistake in the data we used and move on.

While applying my BAD theory, I heard someone say this: "Acknowledge, and move on." It's like a light came on. I thought that was brilliant and one of the most influential messages I had ever heard or used. I think most of my friends want to strangle me when I give them this advice. It sounds so uncaring and dismissive, especially in certain situations, but I have always believed this advice, even when it was hard advice to hear. I truly believe it is what started my path to forgiveness. It's about being in the present—with no past to regret and an open future. How freeing is that? There isn't anything in the past that can be changed, so we need to let it go. Acknowledge it, take its lesson, and then move on. That is what forgiveness is. Forgiveness is not holding on to things that do not bring peace. These things include grudges, resentment, mistakes, guilt, and fear—you name it. Tell me one good thing that comes from holding on to the past? Maya Angelo says, "When you know better, you do better," so by acknowledging the situation as a lesson, we know better. Then we can move on to do better.

When I look back, I can know that everything I did was with the best information I had at the time. If I had known better, I would have done better, which is what I try to do now.

This also helped me learn that I wasn't a sinner. I was just making mistakes.

Good Advice

Some other valuable advice that my professor provided and that I would like to share deals with relationships. My professor said you can't change someone, and if you think you can, you're only fooling yourself. While I knew this, it didn't stop me from staying connected with someone who wasn't for me, but it did get me through breakups with minimal heartache, and I was able to maintain friendships in all of my past relationships.

Another lesson I learned was related to diet. My professor said "If you're not hungry, don't eat." That sounds easy—right? I've never been an overweight person, but like everyone, I have my problem areas, and weight can be a concern. So having this phrase in my head has really helped me. If I am not hungry, and if I find myself eating, I need to remember that something else is going on and that I am substituting food for love. I need to remember God's love.

Below are other words of advice or wisdom that I heard and recorded on my path.

A Dayak proverb says, "Where the heart is willing, it will find a thousand ways, but where it is unwilling, it will find a thousand excuses."

Follow your heart. To do this, whenever you have a decision to make, ask yourself this: "Does this bring me peace?" If not, then don't do it.

My parents always told me this: "If you don't have anything nice to say, don't say anything." While this can sometimes be a challenge in a defensive situation, counting to ten before any confrontation helps to alleviate the regret you know you're going to have later. It also helped me to stop complaining, and why I seem to be a quiet person. I try to reflect before I speak, which helps in my goal of being a good listener.

"Quiet minds cannot be perplexed or frightened, but go on in fortune or misfortune at their own private pace, like a clock in a thunder storm," said Robert Louis Stevenson.

If we can still our minds for a moment, we find God, and He is always giving us opportunities to grow and move forward in this life. But in order to experience God's best, you have to quiet the outside world to hear His voice.

Accept being accepted! I am not sure where I heard this, but it says it all!

The Golden Rule

All of the above lessons were very helpful for me, but the one that was always in my head, that I always applied, and that I now know led me to my goal of forgiveness is the Golden Rule, which says, "Do unto others as you would have them do unto you." Karma means what comes around goes around. This always seemed a little selfish to me, because I sometimes felt I was doing it for my own benefit, but nonetheless, I followed it all of the time. I was able to practice this rule by always trying to give everyone the benefit of the doubt, knowing there was more going on than I knew. The *Course* showed me how to do this more and more.

I always wanted to be heard, so I always tried to stay present and listen when others spoke.

I never wanted to be embarrassed, so I tried to always be empathetic, never embarrass anyone, and accept him or her.

I never wanted others to talk about me, so I never said anything bad about any person.

I always wanted kindness to be shown to me, so I always tried to be kind.

In addressing my obstacles and dealing with my lack of self-confidence, I realized I never wanted to have my feelings hurt or feel judged, so I always tried to never judge others. I also felt that since I had found grace, Jesus, and the Holy Spirit, I wanted this for others more and more.

Laughter

My father said I should be a comedian. I thought that was funny and had no clue what he meant. I can't stand up in front of people, but I think I do have a sense of humor, and I do love to laugh. I love stand-up comedians and sitcoms. Growing up, I liked watching the *Mary Tyler Moore Show*, *I Dream of Jeannie*, *That Girl*, *I Love Lucy*, *Happy Days*, *Laverne and Shirley*, etc. Actually, I pretty much watched any comedy show or movie. I was not a big fan of drama shows, and I never watched horror movies, because I didn't like to be afraid.

Some of the sitcoms I watched when I was very young actually reflect how my life turned out. Looking back, I realize I sort of became these characters. I think the *Mary Tyler Moore Show* was one of my favorites, and I became an independent, working person with many fun people in my life, and I lived in some great apartments. *That Girl* was another favorite. It was about another independent woman living on her own in New York City. Check! I also wanted to live in Jeannie's bottle, but I couldn't pull off the outfit, but many of my wishes have been fulfilled, and my current apartment is small and cozy.

While I can't be a comedian, I do try to use humor or laughter to make others smile and to get them out of their drama or story, so that they can stop taking themselves so seriously for a moment and breathe.

Religion to Spirituality

As a young Christian, I had always felt conflicted about the arguments regarding the theory of evolution. I believed in God, but evolving from the earth also seemed evident to me. I admired Jane Goodall so much, and she pretty much proved the theory of evolution. Through grace, I found peace, and I realized I could believe in both thoughts, because God was in everything.

As an aside, Jane Goodall's foundation was not far from where I lived, so I volunteered there and was able to meet her. It was the blessing of a lifetime, as I found her to be a kind, calm, and thoughtful person. It was like a divine, spiritual connection.

Also through grace, I realized that even things I didn't seem to enjoy—like going to a Catholic school and church—were pushing me forward on my path. In my guilt, fear kept me going back to church. In grace, I found love. I went from focusing on the Crucifixion to focusing more on the Resurrection. In school and church, we read Bible passages and stories mostly from the Old Testament. We were told what these passages meant and how we should apply these lessons to our lives, because as sinners we needed this guidance.

Once I started attending a public high school, I started attending church less frequently. I pretty much stopped going to church after completing all of the Catholic sacramental requirements. While I liked going into churches for some of the peace they brought me, I didn't get anything from the actual services anymore. In grace, I found and started attending Linden Linthicum United Methodist Church. I felt like I needed to be closer to God somehow, so I thought I'd try different traditions, and this church was an excellent start. The pastor there was a big part of that start for me. He didn't make me feel guilty about anything, and he thought I had something to contribute, so I did more for that church than I had ever wanted to do growing up as a Catholic. I set up the church for Sunday service, which I enjoyed because I was alone in God's house, and I was able to talk to Him.

I had been reading the Bible on and off for years, but through grace, I started doing this more often.

The Message—which is a contemporary translation of the Bible—came into my life, and it was so much easier for me to understand. It broke the language down to what I was going through spiritually, and it helped me figure out what I needed to do going forward. I also focused more on the New Testament at that time.

Some messages I recorded from my Bible readings are included in my journal entries below.

Genesis

We should always put God first in everything we do. We shouldn't try to just find Him at church or when we need something.

The Journey Defined

Proverbs
We should assume that we know nothing and reach out to God for all of our answers. This makes us look inside for the answers we seek.

Matthew 5
I need to "rejoice and be glad," because I have a great reward waiting for me in heaven.

This chapter introduces the process of "radical reconstruction";

1. *We recognize we are in need (poor in spirit).*
2. *We repent of our self-sufficiency. We mourn.*
3. *We quit calling the shots and surrender control to God. We're meek.*
4. *So grateful are we for His presence that we yearn for more of Him. We hunger and thirst.*
5. *As we grow closer to Him, we become more like Him We forgive others. We're merciful.*
6. *We change our outlook. We're pure in heart.*
7. *We love others. We're peacemakers.*

Ecclesiastes
The book introduces "the quester," who says we cannot solve anything on our own, so we have to turn to God. Anything else would be insane. It says: "God's in charge, not me. The less I speak, the better. Make the most of what God gives."

Matthew

God doesn't bring light to us. We need to give Him darkness as our light shines back to God.

A simple guide for behavior—ask myself what I want people to do for me. Then grab the initiative, and do it for them.

Luke

Explains that there are no outsiders with God. All are welcomed through Jesus. He says that we are blessed, and when we've lost it all, and when the fears flow freely, joy comes with the morning.

Seek, and I'll find. Knock, and the door will open.

John

He gave His Son, His one and only Son. By believing in Him, anyone can have a whole and lasting life.

Shame is gone!

The friend will come.

If I care for truth and have any feeling for the truth, I will recognize God's voice.

Jeremiah

One of the biggest Bible messages I received came through Jeremiah. This is interesting, because when I was young, my father liked a song from the band Three Dog Night called "Joy to the World," and it started with this line: "Jeremiah was a bull frog." I had always thought that was funny and unusual, but I had no idea that that reference would have such an influence in my life.

One translation of Jeremiah 33:3 says, "Call unto me, and I will answer thee." I first learned about this from the U2 album *All That You Can't Leave Behind*. On the cover, the band was standing in an airport at Gate 33:3, so I looked up the meaning, and Bono called it God's phone number. After that, the number 333 would show up often in my life, and it reminded me to ask God for any answers to my questions. Then other numbers like 11, 111, 1111, 222, and 444, started to show up. I later learned that these are spiritual numbers that demonstrate a divine connection.

Jesus Is Resurrected

In reading the Bible and attending such an inviting church, I started seeing Jesus more through the lens of the Resurrection. I was grateful that Jesus made the sacrifice for our salvation through the Crucifixion, but I wanted some of that Resurrection vibe in my life. I felt it was the "more" I was searching for, so I wanted to find out what this freedom was that Jesus obtained and how I could have it in my life. I just knew these questions needed to be answered for me to find my happiness, and I also knew the answers were in me. The answers could not come from anywhere else.

The *Course* told me this:
"In this world you need not have tribulation because I have overcome the world. That is why you should be of good cheer." (ACIM 2007, T-4.I.13)

"My birth in you is your awakening to grandeur. Welcome me not into a manger, but into the altar to holiness, where holiness abides in perfect peace. My Kingdom is not of this world because it is in you. And you are of your Father. (ACIM 2007, T-15.III.9)

Let's join in honoring you, who must remain forever beyond littleness. Let's join in celebrating peace by demanding no sacrifice of anyone, for so you offer me the love I offer you." (ACIM 2007, T-15.XI.8)

I learned that God gave us Himself. Even when we chose our drama over His love and grace, He was still with us, never forcing us but patiently waiting for us to choose Him.

Fear and guilt prevented me from giving Jesus control over my life, but through grace, I learned to give up some control and let Jesus guide me more and more. I let Him be my example. I learned that fear is always a sign of strain, because what I was doing wasn't lining up with what I really wanted. So before I chose to do anything, I asked how I could find that alignment, and I realized that I have the same place in God's heart as Jesus. We are the same, so I can accept His love and forgiveness and be like Jesus and give love to everyone else.

I was finding happiness, because I started to see I had a purpose. I could fulfill this purpose by showing unconditional love to everyone and still have all the rewards that God's love promised me. What a win! I was so grateful.

When Jesus was hung on the cross, we were saying there was no room for Him in this world, which is how I felt in my guilt—unaccepted and without love. The resurrected Jesus feels no guilt, has no bad habits, and has no fear of death. God wants this freedom for me, so why wouldn't I want it for myself?

Knowing that Jesus is the Way, the Truth, and the Light made me more willing to go to Him. He wants to become the most important person in my life and the greatest love I'll ever know. He wants me to love Him so much that there is no room in my heart or in my life for sin. I just needed to invite Him into my heart.

He goes from heart to heart, asking if He might enter. To those who open their hearts, Jesus promises that "in my Father's house are many rooms." When we make room for Him in our hearts, He makes room for us in His house.

Bono and U2

U2 and their music have probably had the most influential impact in my life. At the time, I didn't know why, and I am sure my friends thought I was obsessed (I was and still am!) But I couldn't stop listening to their music and felt moved more and more. It was one of the healthy obsessions put on my path to guide me.

One of the highlights of my obsession was when the pastor of Linden Linthicum United Methodist Church encouraged me to give a U2 service. Wow! Talking about U2 and God, I was blown away. I am not a public speaker, and the thought of speaking to a group usually terrifies me, but I was so excited when the pastor first mentioned a service with U2 music, because I knew that God was directing me and that He was with me. I was sharing something that had meant so much in my spiritual life, and I knew that my truths would resonate with others and that they would find the same closeness to God that I had felt. It was one of the first times that I had a sense of certainty in my message.

My experience with U2 started when I was in college. A friend of mine invited me to a concert in Washington, DC. I didn't know anything about the band or their music at the time, but I did know that for me, the concert was like going to church – actually better.

The show ended with the song "40," which truly moved me and still does to this day. At the time, I didn't realize it was a psalm. It was the last song on the album *War*, and the band ended their concerts with this beautiful prayer during the *Joshua Tree* tour. Fifty thousand people left that show singing a psalm of belief and hope and the following refrain borrowed from Psalm 6: "How Long to sing this song?" It was a cry in the opening line to the band's other popular song "Sunday Bloody Sunday," which was about the death and violence experienced in Dublin, but it was speaking to me spiritually as a question about how long I would experience my life as an ego rather than the child of God that I truly am. It gave me a sense of unity with others. The voices continued singing as we left the concert and walked to the metro. Even on the metro ride home, people kept singing. This concert was so powerful for me, because so many were joined in truth, and this gave me an internal sense of belonging and even more faith in God.

Here are the words to Psalm 40 in the King James Version:

"I waited patiently for the Lord; And He inclined unto me, and heard my cry. He brought me up also out of a horrible pit, out of the miry clay, and set my feet upon a rock, and established my goings. And He hath put a new song in my mouth, even praise unto our God; many shall see it, and shall trust in the Lord."

These words continue to give me hope and strength through God's love for me. They were the start of my U2 obsession, and I began to listen to all of their music as well as learn everything I could about the band.

I learned that their Christian beliefs are demonstrated in the words to all of their songs and that most of their songs contain at least one verse from the scriptures. Many songs could be interpreted as written about romantic love—similar to my early writings—but I always thought these songs were referring to God. U2 was probably the most influential band in my spiritual journey.

Bono, the lead singer of U2 and the writer of most of the band's lyrics, said, "The soul will be described, but God might not use the people that you expect." For me, He used an Irish rock band to help me hear God's words, and I am glad that I can share my understanding, guidance, song references, and messages with other people.

I have been blessed to work for Bono's advocacy organization, the ONE Campaign, which is an international, advocacy campaign to end extreme poverty. I was able to meet him on a few occasions and can honestly say he is a kind and thoughtful person. I could feel the sense of peace he radiated.

Self-Help Path to Self

Since the Bible told me through Jeremiah and Luke that I could find the answers to my questions, I was more open and willing to ask and receive. I began to open myself to all of the possibilities. Seeking answers, I started following the self-help path. This path continued my habit of always talking to God and my higher Self.

> *The 'He' referred to in the below quote is the Holy Spirit, a friend that is always with me, and it says, if I let go of my perception of situations, I can let Him show me the real reason for everything in my life. I don't know the road to heaven, but I walk with One who does.*

> *The* Course *says the following:*
> *"You will be told exactly what God wills for you each time there is a choice to make. And He will speak for God and for Your Self, thus making sure that hell will claim you not, and that each choice you make brings Heaven nearer to your reach. And so we walk with Him from this time on, and turn to Him for guidance and for peace and sure direction. Joy attends our way. For we go homeward to an open door which God has held unclosed to welcome us. In peace we will continue in His way and trust all things to Him. In confidence we wait His answers, as we ask His will in everything we do. You do not walk alone. His love surrounds you, and of this be sure; that I will never leave you comfortless." (ACIM 2007, W-Epilogue)*

Although I would often ask for material things and solutions to my worldly problems, I also just talked to Him like I had a friend with me all of the time—a friend that I could run anything by.

I think Anthony Robbins provided my first attempt at self-improvement. Through his *Personal Power II:*

The Driving Force I completed a series of written activities that made me search within for my obstacles so that they could be addressed. Since I was associating external values with internal happiness at the time, I did these activities to quell my material desires. I wanted to stop spending carelessly and eat better. Maybe not the best intentions, but it was a start.

Oprah

Then Oprah came into my life. I lived in Baltimore and was in high school when Oprah started doing the news. I remember the ads asking this question: "What's on Oprah?" So I tuned in, and I liked her personality. After she moved to Chicago, I didn't follow her much until she started her "change your life" shows. (A funny side note—I attended one of her shows in Chicago, and the topic was "Inside the Taliban," which was relevant at the time, but I was a little disappointed, because I was hoping for her giveaway show.) However, I was able to shake her hand and see that she didn't just talk the talk but that she also walked the walk. She was very approachable and kind to everyone, and this was something I wanted for myself, so I was appreciative of her example.

Oprah introduced me to so many people that shared spiritual ideas that I already had, but these ideas somehow became unlocked at this time. Because I believed they were shared by all, they showed me more of my higher Self.

The Journey Defined

Below are some of the people who influenced me and samples of their works.

The Four Agreements by Miguel Ruiz is probably the most influential book that kept me moving through the *Course*, because the agreements were the answers to all of my obstacles.

One of the exercises I performed revealed the self-limiting, fear-based beliefs that made me unhappy.

- *I am not good enough.*
- *I'll make a mistake.*
- *I'll be wrong.*
- *I'll be judged.*
- *I'll look bad.*
- *People will make fun of me.*
- *I won't have enough.*
- *I'll be unhealthy and suffer an illness.*
- *I'll say the wrong thing.*
- *I'll hurt people's feelings and upset others, and they won't like me.*

Miguel Ruiz showed me that I need to break these selfish agreements and replace them with the "Four Agreements" below to become stronger.

1. *Don't take anything personal. This is probably the most difficult. I used this whenever I felt any type of confrontation. I would try to see it from the other person's point of view and tried to tell myself it was his or her*

> *fears that motivated him or her, so I shouldn't take it personally. Easier said than done!*
> 2. *Don't make any assumptions. In every situation, we don't know all that's going on, so we should always try to give everything and everyone the benefit of the doubt.*
> 3. *Be impeccable with my words. This wasn't just about always telling the truth to others, although that is important, and I have always tried to never lie. This agreement was more about what we tell ourselves in every situation and about being honest with our intentions.*
> 4. *Always try to do your best. All we can do is try. We don't need to beat ourselves up for making mistakes—as long as we try. BAD, the best available data, has started this process for me.*

These agreements all became a guiding force for me.

Iyanla Vanzant

Another huge influence during the grace period was Iyanla Vanzant. I saw her on Oprah and couldn't believe she had a center in Silver Spring, Maryland—just a few miles from where I lived. I was able to attend a book signing where I met her and felt the connection of truth that we shared.

In her books, she guided me by providing the

questions I needed to ask myself, but she also wanted me to have good thoughts about myself, plan my life, then surrender that plan to God and ask for direction. This is great advice, and I recommend any Iyanla Vanzant book for the seeker.

Elizabeth Gilbert

I was so inspired by Elizabeth Gilbert's book *Eat Pray Love* that I decided to follow her lead and take a year off to write this book. I met her in Chicago at a book-signing event, and when I thanked her for her inspiration, she stopped, took my hand, looked me in my eyes, and thanked me. It was definitely another divine connection on my path.

In her book, she provided the following questions to ask: "In a.m., what do I really, really, really want? In p.m., what made me happy today?"

These were very helpful for me as reminders to touch base with God to see that I was doing what He wanted and to be grateful at the end of the day for what I accomplished.

Gary Zukav

When I first saw Gary Zukav, I have to admit I didn't entirely get his message. But something he said must have stuck in the back of my head, because I would watch any show he was on, and because I picked up his book Seat of the Soul often. He said intentions are the "single most powerful source," because they create the effect. This was another truth that would follow me to the *Course*. It was a natural flow.

Below are some lessons from Gary I wrote in my journal while watching him on Oprah.

I need to align my personality with love, clarity, understanding, and compassion to gain power.

There is no power in fear or in any of the activities that are generated by fear.

Humbleness, forgiveness, clarity, and love are freedom. They are the foundations of authentic power.

When I want something I do not have instead of what I do have, confront it. I should challenge it each time that it comes up by realizing that when it comes up, I am not in the present moment and am not engaged in my present energy dynamic, but rather, I am letting energy leak to a future that does not exist.

Instead of a soul in a body, become a body in a soul. I should look for my soul. This relates to the Course *lesson. I am not a body. I am free, for I am still as God created me.*

Shirley MacLaine

Oprah introduced me to Shirley MacLaine as a spiritual guide. Ouiser was my favorite character in *Steel Magnolias*—one of my favorite movies—so I knew her as an actress and thought it was funny how much I loved and related to her character. She was misunderstood but loved.

The Journey Defined

Quotes from reading Out On A Limb, *by Shirley MacLaine:*

"Lesson: first I am in the light, next the light is in me, and finally me and the light become one."

"I need to love God, love my neighbor, love myself, and love God's work, because I am a part of that work."

"Either I am others' life or death; either I am another's savior or his judge, offering him sanctuary or condemnation."

Dancing in the Light *introduced the following ideas.*

She talks about meeting her higher Self (the HS means Holy Spirit) and is told that "evil" is living backward. (The word "live" is the word "evil" reversed.) We're moving away from our higher Self (God). I am curious if she knows of the Course.

She also talks about a feeling of being unlimited and having no anxiety of time, which are definitely goals of mine.

She experiences something too negative or confusing to deal with but thinks she chose this experience for her own learning, so that knowledge makes it less difficult to cope with. You need to attempt to investigate why events occur so that the pieces can be filled in in the larger picture.

Eckhart Tolle

Oprah had a course for *A New Earth: Awakening to Your Life's Purpose,* by Eckhart Tolle, so I made the commitment to take it, and it was another opportunity to connect with my higher Self, and it really connected me with the *Course*.

> *If the thought of lack of money, recognition, or love has become part of who I think I am, I will always experience lack.*
>
> *My inner purpose is to awaken.*
>
> *Fulfilling my primary purpose is laying the foundation for a new reality, a new earth. Once that foundation is there, my external purpose becomes charged with spiritual power because my goals and intentions will be one with the universe.*
>
> *Awakened doing is the alignment of my outer purpose with my inner purpose.*
>
> *Acceptance means this: For now, this is what this situation and this moment requires me to do, so I do it willingly.*
>
> *I cannot manifest what I want; I can only manifest what I already have. I may get what I want through my efforts, but that's not real. Jesus says, "Whatever you ask in prayer, believe that you have received it, and it will be yours."*
>
> *Jesus told his disciples this: "Heaven is right here in the midst of you."*

I later read *Oneness With All Life: Inspirational Selections from a New Earth*, by Eckhart Tolle. It beautifully summarizes the material from *A New Earth: Awakening to Your Life's Purpose* and seemed to speak directly to most of my obstacles.

> *I have access to God through the present moment, so if I turn away from it, God won't be a reality in my life.*
>
> *Attachment to things drops away by itself when I no longer seek to find myself in these things.*

I need to give up defining myself to myself or to others. I won't die. I will come to life. I shouldn't be concerned with how others define me. When they define me, they are limiting themselves, and it's their problem for not seeing the entire picture. Whenever I interact with others, I shouldn't be there as a function or a role but as a "field of conscious presence."

I don't become good by trying to be good but by finding the goodness that is already within me and allowing that goodness to emerge.

Don't seek the truth. Just cease to cherish opinions.

Joel Osteen

I don't remember how I first learned of Joel Osteen, but his messages also resonated with me, so I watched his show every Sunday. It was my version of church. I bought his books and did all of the lessons he provided.

He started each service with this prayer: "My mind is alert. My heart is receptive. I will never be the same. In Jesus's name, amen." So I stayed focused and always felt guided.

I have over fifteen pages of Joel's messages in my journals, and I want to thank him for each and every one, as they all spoke to and guided me on my journey. It was difficult to choose which ones to share, so at first, I decided to use my logical side and list every fifth one, but then I realized there were so many related to the *Course*—which shows they were placed in my path early on for a reason—so I selected some highlights.

- *Your own wrong thinking can keep you from God's best.*
- *I must look through my eyes of faith and start seeing myself as happy, healthy, and whole.*
- *This could be the day I see my miracle.*
- *What you receive is directly connected to what you believe.*
- *Break the curse. We impact generations to come with the decisions we make today.*
- *You will never go beyond the barriers in your own mind.*
- *If you will change your thinking, God can change your life.*
- *You might be shocked if you really understood how much God wants to bless you.*
- *Your sense of value cannot be based on your achievement, how well you perform, how somebody else treats you, or how popular or successful you are.*
- *Your sense of value should be based solely on the fact that you are a child of God.*
- *We receive what we believe.*
- *God will double any pain into peace, joy, happiness, and success.*
- *Don't settle for mediocrity.*
- *You don't have to live in guilt and condemnation any longer.*
- *What you say in the midst of your difficulties will have a great impact on how long you stay in those situations. (Go to the Holy Spirit first.)*

- *Forgive so that we can be free. A bitter root will produce bitter fruit.*
- *Forgiveness is a choice, but it is not an option.*
- *Don't become trapped in the past.*
- *Even when we are sitting down on the outside, we must see ourselves as standing on the inside.*
- *When you are trusting God, you can be at peace, knowing that at the right time, God will keep His promise—the promise of eternal life with Him.*
- *If it's not meeting a need, turn it into a seed.*
- *Whatever you give will be given back to you. Live to give!*
- *Are you good to people?*
- *Learn to be more than obedient; learn to be willing. (That is all the Course asks.)*
- *It's our faith that activates the power of God.*

Gratitude

I was so grateful for the answers I was receiving and for the feelings of more happiness and peace.

I kept a gratitude journal daily for several years, and I still make sure to remember to be thankful in some way each day. If I have a suggestion for anyone, it is that they do the same because it will transform their lives from negative to positive, even if only in a small sense at first.

I started by writing five things each day in my gratitude journal. Sometimes, it was the same five things from the day before, but it really did adjust my attitude. Other times, it was me talking the talk, and I wasn't necessarily walking the walk. But I could feel a shift occurring, so I made it a habit.

In going through my gratitude journals to determine what I would include for this book, I decided to list only the themes below, because there were 430 Thank-Yous to God, the Holy Spirit, Jesus, and Michael on 846 pages. Let's just say I have been very grateful, and I know this contributes to my peace and happiness.

Here are some of my common themes:

Neville and Phillip—my boys bring so much joy and peace to my life. Whenever they curl up next to me, or I

watch them sleep, or when they are silly boys getting into something they shouldn't, I never get mad. I just smile. Wish I could do that with people all of the time. They definitely are a start to my forgiveness path.

Days when I don't have any plans.

Nice weather, sunshine, being with nature.

Finding things—books, quotes, and the like that make me feel like I am improving my life somehow, whether financially, physically, or my diet.

The good feelings I have when I help someone or make a difference. People telling me how nice or kind I am.

Having time to myself to think and reflect—always looking for ways to improve. I don't think it is meditation or that I am getting answers, but when I look back, it seems like everything is planned for me, and I know it is still happening.

Through the *Course*, I learned that God doesn't want our gratitude but our trust, so we use gratitude to develop our appreciation of Him, which shows we trust Him. I wasn't sure I understood this concept until I applied it to different scenarios in my life. I always felt awkward when someone thanked me after I did something for him or her or gave him or her something physical. I didn't know what to say because it was just something I did, and I think I felt guilty because I felt I had an agenda of wanting to be accepted. But I always feel good when someone trusts me enough to just let me help, maybe by giving directions or taking some advice that I've shared.

I have been fortunate to have many friends in my life, so friendship is another area where I have always been grateful, even when it has been a challenge. I believe people come into our lives for a reason, so I always look for the purpose in my relationships and try to honor that purpose with each person. Most of my lasting friendships began during grace, because with their encouragement and guidance, they kept me on my spiritual path. I think they saw my higher Self before I did. As I mentioned, in guilt, I was kind of faking it, so their encouragement and kind thoughts helped me get to grace, see who I wanted to be, and make it.

Here is a story that reflects how my friends helped me:

I had a friend once tell me that she thought I "put people off" because I appeared to be "too nice." I am not a crier, but I broke down right there because I was so upset. This really struck a nerve, so it had to be important. As I mentioned before, I never want to put people off, and I always try to be kind to everyone I meet. So she had to be wrong, and initially, I felt angry, but because this bothered me, I started trying to figure out why. I came up with two reasons. The first was this: it seemed like she was trying to fix me.

The *Course* says, "To the *ego* it is kind and right and good to point out the errors and 'correct' them." *(ACIM 2007, T-9.III.2)* So knowing that all this was

The Journey Defined

from the ego and fear, I wanted to learn what that fear was. I believed that we don't need to be fixed. We need to be loved, and her comment didn't make me feel loved, and that hurt.

I also know that if something hurts that bad on the outside, there's a deeper inner lesson to be learned. After I let my emotions go and reflected further, I realized she made me feel like I was being a phony, and I think she was right in the sense that I was being a spiritual phony. People always tell me I am a great person, and I want to believe that, but I really don't. I try to be kind, considerate, and compassionate, but the key word is *try*. It doesn't always come naturally to me, and I really wish it did. I would love to be like Mother Teresa, giving up everything to help those in need with complete humility, but that's just not me. I always felt bad about that. Also, in the world of ego, I know that when I do something for someone, I am expecting something in return—maybe acknowledgement, acceptance, or understanding. This desire for some type of return also made and makes me feel guilty.

The funny thing is I was also embarrassed when I was acknowledged. What a mess, huh? I always thought I was a bad person because of these feelings, but the *Course* has shown me that as long as I am here and as long as I am an ego, these thoughts are going to occur, so I need to forgive myself for them and give myself credit for trying. This is all that God asks of me: to try to remember Him and to let go of everything that happens here.

I am grateful to this friend for helping me with this lesson. I grew from this experience, so when another friend said that I had a "gentle empathy and an ability to be present to other people, which is rare and comforting," I actually believed it a little, because I had let some of the guilt go and because empathy was becoming more natural for me. Those words were so nice to hear. I think empathy is what I need to offer my brothers and sisters, and I feel less resentful about doing that, so I think it is part of fulfilling my function.

While I love my friends and need to spend time with them, I am also grateful that I am never lonely when I am with myself. I spend a lot of time on my own, and the only time that I feel like I need to be around someone is when I want to go to dinner or have a glass of wine and catch up. I thought I needed a relationship to feel loved, but I realized that I had one with God who loved me unconditionally, and that was enough.

Another thing that makes me grateful is that children love me. I am not entirely sure why. I never wanted to be a mother, but I love kids, so I am grateful for the ones in my life that have made me feel special at so many points. I think because I am not around them all of the time as a parent, it's easier for me to give them my undivided attention, which, like everyone, is what they really want. This also makes it easier for me to see more of their true personalities, accept them, and respond to them as they are, because I don't see as much of their story. They appreciate this, so we are joined in peace.

I hope sharing my lessons in this book is a good way of passing along my advice to the next generation, so I am also very grateful for this opportunity.

Peace Pilgrim to Pampered Peace Pilgrim

Several years ago, a friend suggested I read the story of Peace Pilgrim, so I found a book about her life, and it changed mine. She didn't write her story, but it was a compilation of her writings—just as this book is a compilation of my journal entries. I think it was another seed planted in me, and I am sure her journey showed up in mine so that I can continue to teach her truth.

The portions I have quoted below are from Friends of Peace Pilgrim's book, *Peace Pilgrim: Her Life and Work in Her Own Words, 1991*. They were instrumental in telling my story. In the copyright section of their book, they provide the following gracious permission:

> "People working for peace, spiritual development and the growth of human awareness throughout the world have our willing permission to reproduce material from this book."

It also says this in the introduction to their book:

> "It is our hope that her words and spirit will continue to inspire. We hope this book will be a valuable resource for these and future writers, as well as an inspiration and encouragement to those who never had the good fortune to meet her." (xv)

I hope that by borrowing her pen and continuing her message, I am honoring her journey through my book.

So what was Peace's story? She was a woman who gave up all of her possessions—she carried everything she owned in a blue smock—and walked across the United States seven times from 1953 to 1981. She walked twenty-five thousand miles during the McCarthy era, the Korean War, and the Vietnam War with her message of peace: "When enough of us find inner peace, our institutions will become more peaceful and there will be no more occasion for war." (xi)

I was and still am inspired by Peace Pilgrim. At first, I admired her ability to give up her worldly possessions, but I thought that would be impossible for me. I had so much stuff I thought I needed, but you will find out later that I am on the path to becoming a minimalist now.

I felt guilty that I didn't share her willpower, but then I realized that was her journey and that I have my own journey. Everyone has a different journey, and none of them really matter. As I said before, the stories may be different, but the goal—peace, forgiveness, happiness—is the same.

It was like she was telling my spiritual journey, but my worldly journey was more along the lines of a pampered Peace Pilgrim. I wanted to be pampered on my path. I wanted to be the Peace Pilgrim that lived at the Westin, a Starwood property, of which I am a member of, and I love their Heavenly Bed! While we differed in stories, it seemed many of Peace's messages were similar to mine, and I felt such a connection.

Like Peace, I believe that we are all one, so when I am peaceful, others feel my peace, and it is extended into a spiritual pilgrimage.

Below are some of her experiences or messages that we share.

***Peace** – "If you want to make peace, you must be peaceful." (p.3)*

"When you approach others in judgment they will be on the defensive. When you are able to approach them in a kindly, loving manner without judgment, they will tend to judge themselves and be transformed." (p.40)

"From all things you read, and from all people you meet, take what is good and leave the rest." (p.130)

***Me** – I was asked once what super power I wanted. At first, I thought it was the ability to speak all languages – to be able to communicate with everyone. Then I decided language wasn't enough, and it was the ability to understand everyone, seeing them for who they really are inside and not the drama they projected—total acceptance, love, peace, understanding of all my brothers and sisters, and magnitude! This started with my trying to apply the Golden Rule.*

I just thought of Paris. I had a vision of sitting in a café with Jesus. We were able to communicate with everyone around us, as they are drawn to us to be one with us for several moments in passing. I should be able to radiate that light wherever I go, because it is at my core, where I am at home. Holy Spirit help me to remember and allow my light to shine forth, loving and forgiving all of my brothers and sisters and myself.

Peace – *"There is no greater block to world peace or inner peace than fear." (p.101)*

Me – *I learned that the Course's purpose is to have no fear.*

Peace – *"When you find peace within yourself, you become the kind of person who can live at peace with others." (p.132)*
"Inner peace comes through relinquishment of self-will, attachments, and negative thoughts and feelings. Inner peace comes through working for the good of all." (p.132)
"Through a great mental effort, you may be able to train yourself not to show fear—but only when you are governed by the divine nature, will you feel no fear." (p.161)

Me – *I feel my path has led me from showing no fear to feeling no fear.*

Travel

Throughout my life, I had always wanted to travel, and I took many vacations with friends and family in my early years. Through grace, I started traveling on my own, and I loved it. Many of my friends questioned my decision. The first question everyone asked was this: "Who are you going with?" They couldn't understand why I wanted to go by myself, and it was difficult for me to explain how much I enjoyed it. I was stepping outside of my box, confronting fears, and learning more about my real Self with each trip. These physical journeys moved me along my spiritual path.

Most of my trips fall into two categories—city meanderings and pampered travel. I was never really into exercise, but I loved to walk, so meandering involved me leaving the hotel and just walking around a city with no real agenda—just seeing what I am meant to see, eating different foods, and sitting and watching the world around me with my journal by my side. I gained so much insight during these trips.

A pampered trip is just that—a trip to a resort with a beach or pool; journals and books by my side; as well as access to spas, massages, and the luxuries that come with hotels.

Below are many journal entries —with some additional commentary—from my travels. As most information is directly from my journals, I hope that my honesty is appreciated and that the messages, experiences, and peaceful moments in my physical journeys are helpful in following my story through grace.

City Meandering

Nice, France – *One of my favorite places that I like to visit often.*

I am sitting at the top of Castle Hill, crying. I wish I knew—really knew—why. I fell and got a little dirty, and the man you pay at the bathroom wasn't very kind, and yet, that's still not a reason to cry. I wish I could get some sympathy at times. Again, I don't know why I need other people to care about me. I know God does—why can't that be enough? Also, I don't always feel like I am sympathetic to others. I need to give to receive. I feel like a lost soul sometimes.

Letting fears go, getting unstuck—now all is perfect, and I trust God and myself that all will be fine.

Another day with endless possibilities. To start, I am at Café Au Long Cours for my pain (bread) chocolate and tea. This café overlooks the market place with its fresh fruits, vegetables, flowers, and spices. The smells are incredible, and there are so many people checking out all of the items. The sun is shining on my face again, and I want to thank God for all His gifts and for me being here to see them.

I have been reading Proverbs, and I have to remember to use them as a guide for my life. When I start thinking negatively or my thoughts wander to fear or lack, God and His words will always be there to help me.

The Café and the Market – Jenn

At a corner café,

Overlooking the market,

So many sights and smells and sounds.

Locals and tourists,

All scrambling for produce, flowers, and spices.

Others, like me, just taking the beauty in.

People of all backgrounds, some with their pets,

Getting along.

I sit here in peace.

As I wandered around, I found a church with an open door, welcoming me in with open arms. I see a crucifix and am reminded of God's gift to the world—His Grace.

The children seem so happy—no cares and no concerns. Can I get back to that place in my life?

The waiters are singing these words: "What do I have to do?" I think they are bored and want customers to come in. I wonder about their lives. Where do they go after their shift? Do they have a family? I want the best for my bored waiters, even if they are making fun of me. I would do the same. I want to stop judging, but now I can laugh about these things. I am sitting here watching people and doing the exact same thing. That's something that makes us one.

I have a smile on my face that may give me away, because I know my waiter just made fun of the couple at the table next to me. He said "here" like he was from the South. Charlie, my waiter, has an attitude. The other waiter is cute and more accommodating. They could be a comedy show.

It took a half bottle of wine for me to get into a Nice spirit and not care what anyone thinks of me. My rude waiter taught me a lot. I need to say "merci."

My waiter just left, and they turned up the heaters in the café. I should order another bottle, but I think I am ready to call it a night. The new waiter is a bit shy.

Chapelle Ste. Rappaporte—My church was open, so I am sitting here now. I think I'll talk to God for a while before dinner. By grace, I give. By grace, I will release.

Found another church named Sainte Rita. There is a man cleaning the wood. Others join me as I sit—just like on the beach. Unity.

Reading in the café—the rain is hitting the awning. People are starting to seek refuge at my café—like I did. They are looking for a dry place to relax and have a meal or drink.

I am finally experiencing the torrential downpours they were calling for, but I am warm, well fed, and still have half a bottle of wine to finish. Rain—it's just water!

The sky and the water are truly magnificent. The view of old and new Nice on either side of me is incredible. See what happens when I let God lead my steps? I need to do this more often in all of my daily journeys.

These are good lessons. I get upset when people are slow, cut me off, or seem rude. They just don't know what they are doing, and who am I to get mad? I had nowhere to go and no time to get there this trip, so why was I in a hurry? God, grant me patience, acceptance of everyone, and love for all. Merci!

I'm looking forward to getting back to see what is ahead for me. Hoping for a move to New York—I think that will happen, so I am excited but want to remember to stay in God's hands and let Him lead me where I need to go. I think that's the best plan I can have forever—stay in the moment.

Dublin, Ireland

Bono/U2 connection.

I want to find love, forgiveness, and God in myself in Dublin.

I hope to remember to ask the Holy Spirit to guide me on this journey, be with me every step, and help me stay in the moment—no fears, no worries, and no guilt.

I'm at St. Patrick's Cathedral. The service has started—needed sanctuary from the rain and cold. A good place to start my journey.

I'm looking forward to settling in at the Clarence (Bono's hotel) and being warm and comfy in Dublin. I'm overlooking the Liffey.

St. Stephen's Green is a beautiful park. Want to come back.

Walked along the Liffey to Phoenix Park, a beautiful park and the biggest park in Europe, according to Noel, my cab driver.

In Eat, Pray, Love *someone says that in each city, there is a thought that everyone shares to reflect the overall feeling, i.e. Paris may be love. Need to figure out the word for Dublin. So far, it's "whatever," because everyone just seems to take things in stride. I'll have to see if that changes.*

I'm at St. Stephen's Green again reading. It's starting to rain, so I took some time to just sit in the rain and reflect on God, knowing my only problem is being away from God. My solution is forgiveness of everything, including myself.

The lady next to me is sitting in the rain reading a paper. Aisling just spoke to me about energy, so I was able to discuss Course stuff with her. I am sure God put us together on these benches for a reason.

I hugged her as we parted. She said I was her oxygen. Lord, let me help others all the time.

Hard Rock. Trabant picture says "God is my copilot."

I need to stop doing things because I worry about what others will think. I need to listen to God and let Him lead me.

It felt nice to follow some of Bono's path.

Will jeggings catch on? I have three pairs.

Took a cab to the airport. Jude Mckenna is from Maryland, Dublin, a small area with saint names as street names.

New York, New York

It gives me peace—always stay at nice hotel.

Beautiful day. Fall is nice in New York—warmer, less crowds.

Through the park, trees reflecting off the pond are beautiful. Fall colors are everywhere.

Café Ruhlmann's for lunch outside in the Rockefeller Center—glass of wine, cheese plate. Tasty.

St. Patrick's Cathedral.

Maybe one day I can live there—by the park.

Feeling a little melancholy today—not sure why. Feel a change in myself—wanting different things but not sure yet what they are.

(New York—I ended up moving there soon after the above trip. Below are entries from my time of living in that city.)

Madison Square Park. Sitting in the park. Realized that no matter how busy a place can be in the city, there is always a place to sit and people to watch. I was going to say interesting people, but we are all amazing as children of God. The more I think about that, the more special I feel—not in a worldly way here but more in the way that I have a purpose that I am able to fulfill for God.

Sitting in the park. Eating a pretzel. An adorable little mouse keeps scaring me. I've given him some of my pretzel, and he is cute. I think I scared him as much as he scared me. I have one piece left, so I hope he comes back. He did—with friends! They jumped out when a bird approached and scared it away. They grabbed the pretzel and ran. This was very entertaining and reminded me why I love it here. It also reminded me of Linda. We were in Washington Square Park on our last visit, and we found some mice friends. It was a fun moment with a fun person.

During the summer of 2010, I started questioning what I wanted to do with my career and myself. I started feeling a calling but couldn't figure it out, so I sat in the park a lot, read the Course more, and kept asking God for guidance. I was getting all kinds of ideas but worried they were from me and not God, so I just kept going, thinking about quitting Turnaround and thinking about going into retail.

Thinking about Eat, Pray, Love. *Where would I go? What would I do? Love that these thoughts are going through my head. They seem like they are coming from God. To my ego, these things sound crazy. I know my friends think I am giving up so much that I have achieved. I will have to sell them on my ideas. Ended up going part time at Turnaround, taking a bookkeeping job at HERE, volunteering, and writing a book. It was a good decision, so it must have come from God.*

Argo Tea—a place that I love to go. Great tea, a place to sit and read and write. I did this often after work. During 2010, I would walk there and read the Course. I was at a point where I was craving it. I couldn't wait to get off work so that I could read. It helped with my anxiety and fears so much. It made me stop asking myself what to do, start asking the Holy Spirit, and trust where I was led. The phrase "decide for me" became something I said frequently.

Charley O's—love sitting in the window with a class of wine. Carla remembered my name after my first visit. She said she remembers the "nice ones." That made me feel great! Reading the Course, I realized I need to be willing to love God. I asked the Holy Spirit for help to put my worldly desires aside so that God is my only thought—not because I think it's what others want to hear or what I think makes me better but because I want to know His love and peace. Just heard

Magnificent by U2 – "I was born to be with you, and ever after, I haven't had a clue." Here in this world, I don't know anything. I am grateful at this moment that I can sit in the middle of this huge city with millions of people and at least think of God and receive messages of truth that give me peace.

Central Park—sitting on the bench in the mall with lunch and a good book. Found a rock in the shade to read on. Maybe I'll take a nap. Someone is preaching. I can't hear exactly what he or she is saying, but I hear God and Jesus's name, so I'll take that as a good thing.

I wrote a prayer. God, Holy Spirit, and Jesus, help me to always ask for the path that I am supposed to be on and help me to correct my steps when I stray. I have many of these prayers written down, and when I write them, I don't necessarily feel guided. But when I look back, I see and know that the Holy Spirit directed me.

There are always so many people in the park, but I always have my own little piece to myself. I learned that this world is just my classroom to learn forgiveness to get me where my real world lies—with God.

Walking around the reservoir – just saw the best real estate in the city—a small bird's nest on a branch over the water in Central Park. It made me smile, and I will look for it every time I pass by. I am sure a sweet family lives there.

Always see birds in the parks in Paris and Nice. They always seem to come around, and I love that. They are calming to me for some reason.

Strawberry Fields. Love the Imagine mosaic. Want to imagine peace, love, and God. I can do that at any time. If I can imagine other "bad" things, why not love and forgiveness? And all that God has to offer? Imagine! In those moments, all is perfect. I always want to remember those moments in times of stress and anxiety. Holy instances are always available. I just need to choose them.

The promenade by the World Trade Center on the Hudson. I can see the Statue of Liberty. Sitting here on Easter. My Course lessons showed me that the Resurrection of Jesus was His example that we will wake from this dream and return to God one day. All of us because we are all children of God—loved and forgiven. Anyone I meet, I have a choice to either crucify him or her or see his or her resurrection. If I judge, I only crucify myself. I have to see everyone as guiltless and loved by God.

Bryant Park. I found a refuge at Bryant Park—a porch with swinging benches and Adirondack chairs where they serve wine and snacks!

St. Patrick's Cathedral. Stop in here often and read from the ONE Faith hymnal.

Work is a big challenge for me, and I don't know why, but I am sure I am here to learn something that will continue the Course I am on. I feel unwelcomed. People aren't nice to one another, and I have never really experienced that before. People can be helpful and friendly, but it seems like they are more concerned with being right and judgmental, which has made it difficult for me. But I think it's because this is what I still need to work on, so these experiences are blessings in disguise.

A little anxiety about where to live. Then realized it doesn't matter, if my purpose is God. He is home. He is in my heart. I can take Him wherever I am. I want peace, and I don't think it's in New York any longer. So maybe Naples. Holy Spirit, guide me.

"Direct My Steps" is in my journal often after I moved to New York. Started turning my path over to God more and more. Hope to continue to do this. I am much less material. Trying to find my spiritual path. Still like nice things—don't get me wrong.

Relationships—I still don't know where I stand on this. I'm very content with my life, and I don't see someone fitting into it, but I think I should just keep an open mind. I want to want to keep God first, and I hope that if I do get into a relationship, that can still happen. I need to turn this over to God so that He can guide me. The only time I feel like I need someone is when I want to catch up with a friend. I have this often, so I think I'm covered, but it may be nice to have someone to share this with more often. Again, I'll give it to

God. He's done pretty good so far.

I Forgot to Look Up – Jenn

As I move throughout the day,
So focused on the next thing to do,
I feel I have put blinders on
And am missing the panoramic view.

Hampered by my narrow vision,
Of an ego world of tasks.
Looking for a bigger picture,
Of a path that God has paved.

Fear, anxiety, boredom, and guilt surround me,
As I choose this worldly road.
My mind needs to wander up to heaven,
Surrendering all, give God my load.

Connected – Jenn

Look into the core,
We're all the same.
Created as one
Under His name.

Connected in peace,
Connected by love,
Here, now on earth,
Not just from above.

Forgiveness is needed.
Acceptance of others,
Connected to Him,
All one as brothers.

His love is equal for all.
He calls each to come.
The choice is ours:
To be separate or one?

Joined in peace,
Connected by love,
We have these in common.
He is enough.

Paris, France – *I felt like I belonged there for some reason. I still do and feel there is a calling for me to go to France. I think God started me on that path when I decided to take three years of French in high school. Of Course, I didn't see it then, but it was a start and more proof that I was being guided.*

I haven't been thinking about God much today, so I think I will take this moment (a holy instant) to think about Him and how blessed I am. I am sitting in an incredible place with all of my brothers and sisters from all over the world. I want them all to feel the peace that I feel at this moment—when we are all free with no quilt, fear, or lack. There is no judgment of anyone, no past to worry about, and no future to be anxious about—just now where we all love each other, especially with ice cream on the way.

I followed my feet to one of Your "houses" named Sacre Coeur. There is a small crucifix, but I am looking at Jesus with His arms wide open and a huge heart. Let me know Your heart, Jesus. Let me be Your heart and do what You call me to do. I love You and want to be You. Give me the strength and courage to follow Your path. Help me to forgive as You forgave, love as You have loved, and not be concerned with the ways of this world. I seek my Father's home.

Reading A Moveable Feast. *"Although it was always Paris, and you changed as it changed."*

Remembered my meditation from before about me and Jesus sitting in a café in Montmartre. Want to think about that while I am there later.

A woman asked me to walk her across the street. Her hands were soft. I thought it was another trick like last year, but it wasn't, and I felt connected to someone for a moment. I like helping others and want it to happen naturally like that more often.

Walked to Notre Dame. Inside looking at the statue of Mary over Jesus's body again. Reminding myself I am not a body but a spirit like Jesus.

Thanked God that I am shedding my ego ways and asked for help to not judge my brothers and sisters for their need to want to be heard and noticed. I know this is something still in me that I need to forgive, which is why I see it so much in others. I want to remember my lesson today and try to see Christ's face in others and when I look in the mirror tonight.

On this journey, I need to remember to keep choosing Him as my companion instead of the ego. I can't hold on to both, or I will try to go in different directions and lose my way. I've been feeling this lately, so I am asking Jesus to stay with me and help me be in this world but know where I belong.

Jesus needs me as much as I need Him, so, Holy Spirit, help me to remember that I am helping Jesus when I let these thoughts of the ego go. He doesn't want me nervous, anxious, fearful, or worried, so, Holy Spirit, help me think of Him when I do these things with others and help me know I am united with my brothers and sisters in this also.

I realized I need to forgive time. That is what gets me anxious and worried. Need to stay in the moment, take Jesus's hand, and do what He needs me to do, not all of the things I think I need to do. Take a breath! That sounds like a great plan, so I hope to remember it and follow it.

Walking to the Arc de Triomphe, I was a bit miserable with the wind and the rain. I need to forgive my hair. Worrying about it and what people think of me is draining and takes me away from Jesus's hand.

Everything seems to be bugging me today—smokers, kids with pigeons, and the gravel. I am trying to see things through Christ's eyes, but I am being very judgy. Help me, Holy Spir-

it, to know we are all with God at peace. Let me want that for the boys throwing gravel at the pigeons now. I left, and I am still a little bitter. Holy Spirit, Jesus, and God, help me!

Took the metro to Montmartre. I am sitting in Sacre Coeur again. Felt like I needed it. I wasn't here long before I started to cry. I am not sure why, but I asked Jesus to take my hand and help me get rid of all the things that don't matter—hair, money, food, weight, and work anxiety. I may be crying because I felt guilty about how I responded today to the little boys or the wind and rain. I know I am forgiven, but I don't want to judge, and I can't stop. I can't see everyone as forgiven, and I want to know how. Help me, Jesus!

Help me give up guilt so that I can stop judging and find your peace.

Thank You for allowing me to cry with You, Jesus. I didn't need anyone else, and I feel like some weight has been lifted. Help me to remember this moment, and let everyone know the peace that I feel.

I feel much better. Will go to Sacre Coeur again tomorrow!

Bought a card of the picture of Jesus from the church, so He is with me spiritually and physically as I sit in the café in Montmartre. I want to let Him be with me always and remember He is there! Forgiveness is our universal communication that I envisioned, and I am feeling less judgy now. Yay!

Prayer on back of card by Saint Thomas Aquinas: "O Sacred Banquet, in which Christ is received, the memory of His Passion is recalled, the soul is filled with grace, and the pledge of future glory is given to us."

This is one of the first trips I wasn't anxious to go home. I always have a great time wherever I go, but I usually wonder how I will fill the time. I think I am starting to learn how to take things as they come and stay in the now. Part of me is starting to be a little sad to be leaving tomorrow, but I know I'll be back and that there is such potential in what is to come in my life. I just got excited thinking about it.

Pampered

I love to be pampered, and I think my first true experience of this started with Oprah's suggestion of Miraval Spa and Resort – Life in Balance in Arizona.

As we entered, we were told the "i" in Miraval means "I." All to think about—if we don't take care of ourselves, we can't do anything for anyone else.

Laying out by the pool. Very calm. Relaxed. See humming bird. I want to eat healthy, drink plenty of water, get moderate exercise, and just relax.

Horseback riding. Copper. Very sweet. Able to ride many terrains. A long ride with very beautiful scenery. Very peaceful.

What would I do if I didn't care what others thought?

Life in balance. I hope to maintain a balanced life—wherever that leads.

Atlantis Nassau, Bahamas

Some friends and I went to Atlantis many years ago. We had such a good time, and it was the epitome of being pampered. I bought a time-share there and have been back many times since. My goal each time is to relax and connect with God, and that goal is always realized.

Walk to spa. Love the spa smell. Massage=Heaven. Eighty minutes of relaxation.

Atlantis is incredible. Treated like royalty!

I love paradise. I could get used to this.

Reading Eat, Pray, Love. *It's making me think. I am ready to do something. I am not sure what yet, but I am open to what will come.*

Thought about God and the Holy Spirit. Need to ask God to guide me in everything that I do. Felt at peace for a bit and want to find that peace more every day.

Woke up. Thought about God and the Holy Spirit. Not as afraid to see the "real world" after reading The Shack. Curious how God will show up for me.

Woke up early again. Thinking about why I let things upset me. Asked the Holy Spirit for guidance.

Read through some other trips. Glad I keep this journal and document my trips.

Sacred Springs Retreat in California

Walking in the airport. Had a good feeling that everything is and will be good. I won't worry anymore about weight, health, or money. Know it will all be OK.

Lunch. All natural and very yummy. I have been thirsty, so I will drink a lot of water. The creek sound is so soothing!

It's beautiful here!

Reading the Untethered Soul *about keeping the heart open. When I am anxious, upset, or unhappy, I need to realize they are past hurts, pain, and guilt. I must let them pass so that I don't expend any unnecessary energy. Spiritually acknowledge and move on.*

I am feeling abundant and hope this continues.

My belly is full of good things, and I am getting tired. I think I'll sleep well here with the sound of the water. Although I have had a lot of water also. The bed looks comfy!

Just be…
- *Open to all possibilities*
- *Quiet*
- *Still and know that I am God*
- *A channel for nature and God to flow through me*
- *Confident in who I am and what I can be and have*
- *Healed*

God Take…

Worry about what others think—I am feeling that now since I am the only one here, so I am not feeling guilty. Blockage—God punishing me if I was bad growing up. I know this isn't true and need to let it go.
- *Not feeling worthy*
- *Doubt about my future*
- *Guilt about wanting more and more*
- *Feeling of others not understanding or accepting me. Not being able to be myself*

- *Worries about health*
- *Thoughts of boredom*

When I think of these things, I am happy…
- *Getting rid of things*
- *Having nice things*
- *Dinner and wine with friends*
- *Being able to tip well for services I receive —massages, cleaning, being served at hotels. I think this is the purpose of me becoming a pampered Peace Pilgrim.*
- *Not working—not being around gossip and negative talk that I judge*
- *M&M World in Las Vegas—comfy hotel bed in Vegas*
- *Being natural—no vitamins or pills*
- *No worries about eating or spending*

Ideas…
- *Consulting career so I can make my own schedule*
- *I really don't want to work, and I don't want to feel guilty about it. I would like to volunteer to do something with children somehow, just hang out with friends and listen to them and be there for them*

I am not happy at work. There is so much negativity, and no one seems happy about anything. People can be so mean to each other sometimes and complain often. I feel they judge everything and everyone. The gossip and complaining really weighs on my soul. I don't want to be a part of it, but it's hard to avoid and difficult to make lasting friendships, because I try to avoid it. I want to find peace and not have these thoughts and blockages. Help me with this! Let them pass through me so that I can be present and know that my future doesn't have to be what has passed.

This is my dream, and I want it to be happy. No negative thoughts, no guilt, no problems, no time, and no more job.

My solution is that I want to leave. Guide me, Holy Spirit.

A great night's sleep after a bath with Epsom salts and lilies.

Saw a hummingbird. Heard the creek. Smelled various flowers. Felt happy and content with nature. So quiet and peaceful and not feeling any boredom so far. I have let some mosquitos "bug" me, but that was brief. Overall, I am feeling good!

Thank You, Holy Spirit. Please keep taking my dark thoughts from me, so I only see, hear, and feel the peace and happiness that God offers.

"I Just Need a Place for My Mail to Go." – how I feel about where I live. Lately, haven't thought about one place that is necessarily for me. I think I just want to roam to wherever I am led.

New York still gives me the most smiles, but I'll see. M&M World in Las Vegas just made me smile again (I love M&Ms).

Funny, the phrase "more and more" keeps showing up in my thoughts. I feel it more inside than ever before. I am healed.

A leaf fell in the creek in front of me. I watched it, but I looked ahead to see where it would go. Then it stopped and is just sitting on some old branches, and then I realized it doesn't matter. It just is.

My mosquito bites from earlier seem to be gone now, so I am happy. Then I just got more and scratched, so I have red marks on my arm, but I want to be happy and let this blockage pass. Help me release bugs.

I am bugging myself by not letting go of my hang-ups. I had faith earlier as I watched the bites come, grow, and disappear. I thought the universe had sent me signs, but now I am doubting again. I need to remember the universe didn't send them. I did, and I want to not give them any attachment. They just are, and this too shall pass. All is well!

Thank You, Holy Spirit, for an incredible meal. Feeling full and not thinking ahead to the next meal. Wanting to do this more and have more and more healthy experiences.

Took a nap. A lot of thoughts. Conclusion. The phrase "it just doesn't matter" came to me. (Remember this from Meatballs?)

Nothing has happened. I don't need to think about it. Let it all go.

I want to be happy now and go from there, knowing I'll always be happy. I have no problems.

Sitting by the stream. Beautiful but let bugs bug me again. How can I be one with nature, if bugs bug me?

Meditation—don't judge my thoughts. Just let them flow —come and go.

Thought this morning. The truth store is open, and I am ready to buy.

First—stay in the present. Don't think about the future, the next meal, or worry. Trust all will happen as it's supposed to, and it will be perfect.

Thought this morning. I am the cause and effect, if my goal is happiness. Both are the same. I have no problems that are not already solved.

The Raj – Fairfield, Iowa

Several years ago, I started doing Transcendental Meditation, and the Raj is an Ayurveda Health Center in the city of Maharishi Vedic. The peacefulness was incredible!

Giddy at arrival. A white, warm, and welcoming bed in a lovely room.

Nothing to do. No expectations. Letting fears go. Unstuck. All is perfect, and I trust God and myself that all will be fine.

Creation is finished. My ideas for freedom have already occurred, and I want to collapse time for them to be realized, and I can do that by staying in this moment.

All questions have already been answered. Holy Spirit, help me hear You when You answer me. Thank You for all the answers You've given me to make me happy.

Other Significant Trips in My Journey

Honolulu, Hawaii

I went to Hawaii for the final night of U2's *Vertigo* tour. Two significant events happened with this trip. First, I think this is where my idea of being a pampered Peace Pilgrim started. Oprah did a show at that time where she gave people one hundred dollars to pass along to someone else, so I was inspired to give a woman who made beautiful ornaments a lot more than she was asking. It was the best feeling, and I want to do it all of the time. I want to be pampered, and in my journey, I want to be generous to those that assist me, because I am truly grateful for what they do.

Secondly, before leaving for this trip, I decided to leave the credit union to work for a nonprofit. I decided I wanted to work for Bono and found out he had a nonprofit in Washington, DC. They were looking for a director of finance, so I applied. At the concert, I felt I would get the job, and I did.

Here are more journal entries:

"Mahalo" means "thank you." Royal Hawaiian is very nice. Received leis at arrival. Pink everywhere. The trees are beautiful.

Concert day! Head to concert. Can't wait to see U2. Had a Li-Hing margarita. It was really good. U2 was everything I could imagine. So good. Started with "City of Blinding

The Journey Defined

Lights." Then did "Elevation" and "Vertigo." The place was moving. So powerful.

Ended with singing "All I Want Is You" after playing with Pearl Jam, "Rocking in a Free World," and Billy Joe from Green Day. "The Saints Are Coming."

Sang "Window in the Skies." So good!

It was an awesome show. I am so happy to have been there to see the final performance of Vertigo.

Gave Makhleka one hundred dollars. So nice. She wanted to know "where the money came from." Too cute. It felt good to help her.

Watched sunset.

I had a nice time. I really enjoyed the concert. U2 is so awesome. I am hoping I'll find a new job soon, and I am feeling confident in my decision. The more I get away and have time to think about things, the more I know I am doing the right thing. Thank You, God!

La Paz, Bolivia, and Oruro, Bolivia

I sponsored a little girl named Jacqueline in Bolivia through Save the Children, and I was fortunate enough to go there to meet her.

More examples of how my pampered Peace Pilgrim idea could come to fruition:

Flight to La Paz. Business Class. Very nice. Salmon for dinner. Warm nuts and mushroom soup.

Met Juan, the driver provided by Save the Children. Very

nice. Glad I had a ride that was so friendly. A lot of dogs running around.

La Paz is in a deep valley. Mountains surround it—beautiful!

Arrive at Hotel Europa. Very nice. Took a little nap. Then walked around and found a street fair and picked up all my gifts and a couple scarves for me.

Back to the room for some more rest and relaxation. Glad the altitude isn't bothering me too much but can definitely feel it. I think I will take a bath and chill so that I am ready for tomorrow.

Juan and Laura, the coordinator of Save the Children, picked me up at 7:30 a.m. Heading to Oruro, I asked Laura a lot of questions. Want to follow Bolivian election. Arrive at Save the Children office. I met Augusto.

Went to school. Met Juan, Tatiana, and Brian. Toured school with teacher and principal. Broke strike to come for me.

Jacqueline and her family showed up. She made me a purse and cake. I felt like a rock star, but they are the incredible ones. Her mom, Nancy, has cancer. Her brother works in sewage and is going to school to help his mother and grandmother. Jacqueline helps her mother sweep streets and loves school.

Able to leave donation for a bookshelf and some books. They called it a "library." Hope to do more of this going forward.

Had a yummy lunch with Juan and Laura at Pasta Primavera. Had to leave for La Paz because of protest troubles that could have broken out.

The kids were cute and asked how to say the words "thanks" and "friend" in English. Arrived back at hotel. Upgraded to a suite.

Went to Save the Children office. Met Laura, Carmen, and Gary, the director. All appreciated my sponsorship and made me feel like I was doing a lot.

Walked around La Paz. Bought a lot of scarves. Some are gifts, and some are for me. Saw a couple of protesters but nothing scary. Found out there were problems in Oruro last night from the protestors. A few deaths. Now I know why Juan and Laura cut the visit short. They were trying to keep me protected. Good that we left when we did. While violence surrounded, I felt protected and loved on this trip. Amazing!

Acca, Ghana, and Lagos, Nigeria

As an employee at the ONE Campaign, I was able to travel to Africa. We were there to see how PEPFAR (President's Emergency Plan for AIDS Relief) funds were being utilized. There were many inspirational stories. I thought this would be a trip where I felt sorry for others or guilty for what I had. But I just ended up feeling blessed for each experience.

Airport early. Waiting for the gang to show up. I want to take each moment as it comes, not think about the past or too far into the future.

I want to find silence and awareness in all things at all times.

I will try to spend time with coworkers, giving them my full attention on this journey we are about to share. Be present!

I want to find God there, to see and know love and forgiveness in everyone and everything at all times. I am asking the Holy Spirit to be with me and help connect me with God on this journey and on my greater journey back to my Father.

African Regent Hotel. Very nice and modern. Waiting to feel like I am in Africa. Can't believe I feel pampered here. Thank you, Holy Spirit.

Visited a cocoa farm named Cocoa Arabapo to see how cocoa is picked, fermented, and dried.

Everyone thinks I am quiet, but I just like to listen and reflect, and I don't always feel like I fit in—too many people trying to get attention. I just want to blend in.

Today is my day to represent the ONE Campaign, so I am asking the Holy Spirit to be with me today so that I have no fear, because God loves me and because there is no fear.

Arrived at village for bed-net demonstration.

I hung two bed nets in a woman's home for a mother and daughter.

Leave for school district in St. Agnes in Maryland. Go figure—I was born in the St. Agnes Hospital in Baltimore, Maryland. The kids are amazing and they shared their lessons.

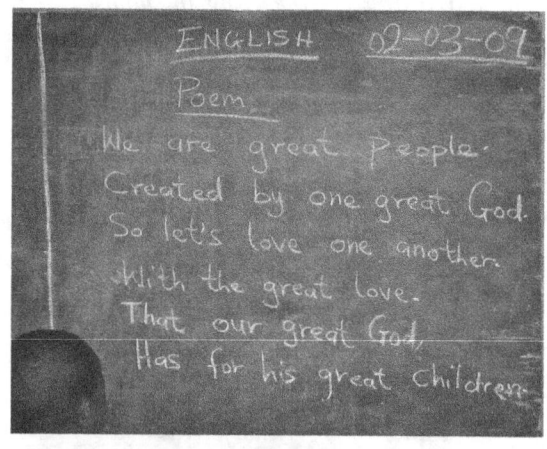

Bariga slums and new market. Women market owners. Water is a blessing.

Met Ademola. Happy to have gutter improvements. Two children – her daughter is seven, and her son is five. Living space was the size of an average American bathroom. Able to leave contribution for rent for a larger place. Felt good to help but want to do more. Beautiful woman with a beautiful heart. She gave me a hug. I felt a connection!

Lagos University Teaching Hospital. Patients living with AIDS.

Arrive in the city of El Mina. Coconut grove on the beach. Had a nice dinner by the beach. Feet in the water of the Atlantic Ocean off the African coast.

Heading to canopy walk. Kaleum National Park was incredible! Scenery is beautiful. The castle in El Mina is the oldest stone building in tropical Africa. Slave trade. Difficult to believe.

God was everywhere on this trip! I wish that I had remembered this more. I will spend the day on the beach, relaxing and reflecting on the trip.

Guilt Obstacles Addressed Through Grace

With grace came the realization of two worlds, internal (self) and eternal (Self). My struggle before grace was caused by guilt and fear from an external world that I was creating myself. In grace, I started to learn what my fears were and how to address them. I learned that I get what I expect. If we are always afraid of something bad happening, it usually will happen.

Why do we do that? We create our outer world with these thoughts, which is why there is so much pain and suffering in the world. If we channeled our energy into hope, peace, and happiness, we would see our world change.

I learned that God wanted me to know love and be happy, and only by fulfilling this function would I find peace. There is no other way, so every time that I choose whether I will fulfill my function, I am really choosing whether I will be happy. With this knowledge and accountability, I started to feel empowered to have and be more and more. All of the answers were within me.

Since I've shared all of my grace lessons, below are some conclusions to where I was with the obstacles I tried to overcome on my journey. Basically, I realized every obstacle was a form of fear, and since the opposite of fear is love, I wanted love. So that is what I sought and was provided with when I called on God.

Lack of Money Revisited

In guilt, I always thought I needed money and things to make me feel important and to have people accept me, and there was never enough money to accomplish this goal.

While I still have thoughts of lack from time to time, the lessons below remain in my consciousness. I was able to turn things around. I supported myself, had money in the bank, and had no debt. Now I want to have enough money to do the work that makes me happy, and I want to become a pampered Peace Pilgrim. I feel I will reach this goal, because it is God's will.

Through grace, I was introduced to other teachers, such as Suze Orman and Maryanne Williamson—who helped me understand the role that money should play in my life.

Suze Orman

I read many of her books, and while she helped me get financially organized, it was her spiritual messages that had a more lasting impact. Basically, she said money doesn't make me who I am. I can find love and peace regardless of what is in my bank account.

In addition, she always ended her show by advising that we put "people first, then money, then things." This showed me that my intentions are important, so I always need to investigate what they are and how they bring me peace so that I am doing the right thing with my money.

Marianne Williamson

In her book, *The Law of Divine Compensation: On Work, Money, and Miracles*, she shared that the world is an abundant place and that I deserve the abundance. And if I don't think I do, it's my own fault.

My new truths are the following:
1. I have more than I'll ever need.
2. I don't need things to make me happy.
3. I have control of my money.

Messages I received from Marianne Williamson:

The universe will never support me in my attachment to things and wanting them in a certain way. Love is not form – it is content. God may not give me what I want how I particularly want it, but He gives me love in all things that do come my way.

Abundance comes from surrendering my talents and asking they be used by God to bring peace to the world.

Money comes from the universe, not just because I have a material need, but by the energy of righteousness, which means 'right use' of the mind, and the only right use of the mind is love.

I don't need to struggle in order to experience abundance. When I do, it interferes with the natural magnetism that otherwise brings abundance forth.

I am empowered not because I have money but because with that money I can help empower others. I shouldn't be coming from a 'get' mentality, but just allow the universe to flow through me and use me in a way that serves a greater good.

Physical Body

Most of my life, I have been pretty thin, but in guilt—like everyone—I always worried about my weight, what I was eating, and how it impacted my appearance or health. This always produced some type of fear or anxiety that I didn't want in my life.

I learned in grace that God wants love and happiness for me, so I tried to figure out how I could obtain peace with regard to food. Everyone knows that overeating isn't about food but about something that is going on inside. Our thinking about it all of the time and our worrying creates fear, so if we're not thinking about it and not letting it control us, it's easier to overcome. Oprah recently joined Weight Watchers and has had success. I think this is because it is a lifestyle change that takes our own thinking out of the process by using points so that we're not as obsessed with and living in fear of food. It becomes more of a natural process.

The stress-management teacher I mentioned earlier said that when you go to eat something, you should ask this: "Am I really hungry?" If not, don't eat. Do something else as a distraction. I thought this was good advice, but I needed more. Kenneth Wapnick—a follower of the *Course*—in his book *Overeating: A Dialogue*, provided the addition of asking the Holy Spirit for help in these moments. So now if I ask, "Am I really hungry?" and if I say "no," then I should ask the Holy Spirit how I should proceed and wait for the answer. This keeps me more present with food, so I am not thinking about what I ate or about what I am going to eat with any regret, because I am doing it with God and am giving Him any fears that I have. I am at peace.

I have also always believed that I should eat everything in moderation. So if I am really hungry, I try to figure out what I am hungry for, and that's what I eat—whether it's a salad, pizza, or ice cream. By allowing myself to eat anything whenever I want, and by trusting it's the right thing, I don't worry about food so much, and maintaining a normal weight has become much easier.

My overall health has been a challenge throughout my life. As I mentioned, I had a heart murmur when I was young that required open-heart surgery. Also, at a relatively young age, I needed to have a hysterectomy, so menopause came instantly, and my body has been rebelling ever since. This sudden change in hormones created hair, weight and other health issues, which unfortunately also impacted my vanity. It has probably been one of the biggest challenges I have had to face, and not necessarily because of the physical body issues, but because it brought with it a fear that I thought was out of my control. I felt my faith was being tested. I know my anxiety ultimately comes from a fear of death, which was strong in my guilt, but in grace, I learned that there is no eternal death. Jesus did not die! I realized that this is true when I look within and see Him. The Resurrection of Jesus changed my perception because it proved that I will wake up from this dream and return to God one day—just as He did. When I learn to make Him important, I will never see death, and this thought has helped lessen my fears, take health issues as they come, and find peace that my issues will end eventually. As the adage goes, "this too shall pass," and that goes for everything that worries us or causes any anxiety.

Judgment

So in grace, I tried to see everyone, including myself, as guiltless. I learned that my feelings of lack created my judgments, so with God's love now in my world and with learning that there is no lack, I was able to eliminate some of my fears.

I was still judging, but I started trying to see things from a different perspective. I learned that we all do things for two reasons—to find love or to remove fear. This helped me give others the benefit of the doubt. When someone is bitter or mean, it's because he or she is afraid or lonely, so I need to offer this person love and acceptance. Anything else will make things worse.

I know we all judge everything and everyone all of the time. Looking out at others is easier. We make them wrong and ourselves right. It makes the problem outside of us instead of in us. It takes away our responsibility to deal with our own stuff. I heard someone say that when we point a finger, there are three pointing back at us. What we judge in others is really what we need to correct and forgive in ourselves. I asked myself what my judgments of myself were, and I was able to address them.

As I observed my judgments more and more, I learned that most of them occur when I am out in the public, and they relate to the idea that people are thoughtless, uncaring, rude, and inconsiderate. It's usually because they don't see me, cut me off, or stop in front of me. First off, I know it's not intentional, and I am certain it's not spiritually intentional. It's my stuff showing up—such as feeling unworthy. Now I laugh at it more and let it go.

I also realized that everyone wants to be heard, seen, accepted, noticed, and the like, but unfortunately, they seek these things through creating drama. They do things to be acknowledged, and it can be in a good way or in a bad way. Just accept them, and that provides the love they need. Overlook the drama, and know they just want love. So why not give it to them rather than judge them? This can be difficult. My ego will always judge, but my spirit knows better, so I just keep trying to remember this lesson as often as I can.

I try to ask this: "Am I a blessing to those around me or a burden? Do I lift guilt from them, or do I lay it on them?" I am here to be a channel of God's grace to the world and to release everyone I come into contact with from their guilt, especially from the guilt I have laid upon them.

During grace, some new truths became evident. I wrote about them in my journal.

"Good luck" is now "good thoughts." There is no luck. What is just is.

- *I want to be happy, and when I am, it is more natural for me to want to give to others. I need to find my happiness, and it will be extended to others naturally. I don't need to feel guilty about this.*
- *I don't feel lonely because I know God is always with me. I think I have had more faith than I gave myself credit for. I've felt blessed, but I thought I, or my ego, was making it happen, but it was the Holy Spirit.*

Fortunately in guilt, I had always had a feeling that there was another way. I knew it, but I would get frustrated when I couldn't see or obtain the alternative. My frustration came from not knowing the alternative was God, and this came in grace. I started to surrender and undo my story, which led to the *Course*. I was very happy, but I knew there was still more, and I was coming from a place of more consciousness and awareness—a place where I was ready to receive and give. This led me to forgiveness, and from fear to peace and love.

PART 3

Forgiveness

Chapter 6

It's Not a Story – It's Peace

It is not a story anymore! I just need to be in this moment with my goal of peace and freedom!

I love puzzles, and I saw my life in this respect. All of the pieces from my story that I had recorded in my journals from guilt through grace were coming together to complete my picture of forgiveness, and with that, my ego and my worldly goals were being realigned to my spiritual goals. Along my path, I had found many other peace pilgrims, like Bono, Oprah, and Peace Pilgrim, using their stories, so I wanted to become a peace pilgrim, and I realized it was OK to be a pampered one. I don't have to feel guilty about wanting this for myself, because it makes me happy and brings me peace, and I want to share that energy with everyone.

Surrendering through grace, letting go of fear, and looking for love allowed me to become aware of my eternal Self, and everything seemed to come together "more and more"—a phrase that became a thought I always have now because it is what I expect in life. I try not to figure out what it means in my ego world and continue to surrender to God's plan for what I will receive, because He has so much more planned for me than I could ever imagine for myself.

The *Course* told me the light has come. I have forgiven the world. I am healed and healer, peace and peacemaker, and happy and happiness to all. I have the power right now to be completely at peace and to offer peace to everyone. Jesus takes my hand and guides me toward the light and truth.

In grace, I realized all my obstacles are some sort of fear, and I was able to get to the heart of every problem by asking this: "What am I afraid of?" The answer was this: "You think you are separate from God." Since I now knew He never left me, I would ask Him how I could solve whatever problem I was going through and wait for the answer. My fear went away because I knew there was an answer to my question, and I felt loved and free. This book proves my lack of fear, as I would have never opened myself up to this level in the past, and I feel so blessed for this opportunity.

To find peace and forgiveness, we need to give up our story, so I will use my more current journal entries as a means for me to continue to undo my story—to continue to self-purge.

One Thought – Jenn

All I need to know is in one thought.
So easy yet I can't seem to remember that one thought.

*I let the vast amount of other thoughts take hold,
    manipulating me with what I don't need to know and
    what causes me fear, anxiety, and guilt.
All the while, one thought can bring me only love and
    peace—one thought.
You love me.*

Ego Growth

- *I thought God was testing me all of these years.*
- *Actually, my ego is testing me. There is not a test
    from God. He loves me, no matter what I do
    —whether I pass or fail in the ego's eyes.*
- *If I trust, forgive, know myself, know peace, and
    am open to the Holy Spirit's guidance, my mind is
    willing to receive, shortening the bridge to unity
    with God, Jesus, Michael, the Holy Spirit, the angels,
    and the saints—all those helping me to find peace.
    I am not separated from them. We are one.
    By asking the Holy Spirit for help, I am removing
    the ego and my control over everything. I need
    to do nothing. After that, knowing the Holy Spirit
    will take me where I need to go.*

Sitting in the courtyard at lunch. This is my lesson for today: let me recognize the problem so that it can be solved. The problem is separation. I realize I try to relate to others to forgive them, but I think I need to start trying to see them as without a body and ego at all and as loved and accepted by God. They are just here to work through their dream, and I don't have to do anything for them—just know it's a dream for all of us.

Now. Meditation. Mindfulness. More inner work. Connecting with the mind of God, who doesn't care about my story and only wants my happiness, which is coming home to Him. All I have to do is let Him guide me! Stay present. The past is the guilt and cross story. The future is grace. No past. Forgiven. No story. Resurrected. This is just a dream I am creating. I am learning to receive peace, love, and forgiveness and to give.

Each instant is a clean, untarnished birth, in which the Son of God emerges from the past into the present. And the present extends forever. It is so beautiful and so clean and free of guilt that nothing but happiness is there. No darkness is remembered, and immortality and joy are now.

Help me feel God's love and know what that means while I am in a body. Let me let You guide me, trusting I am following Your voice and not my ego.

I want peace, but now I want it how I think it should be, so let me want it and accept it how You offer it.

No littleness. Only God's magnitude for me. All things are possible.

No guilt. No fear. No worry. No doubt. No anxiety.

It's OK to have impure thoughts. Don't keep them. Give them to the Holy Spirit, and have no guilt or fear because He does not judge you but accepts you as you are. Nothing I do in this dream matters.

> *"To forgive is merely to remember only the loving thoughts you gave in the past, and those that were given you. All the rest must be forgotten."(ACIM 2007, T-17.III.1)*
>
> *I need to grasp the habit of referring everything to the Holy Spirit rather than trying to figure it out myself with the help of my ego, and everything would simply fall into place. This alone would set me free.*
>
> *The Holy Spirit takes what is going on in this world to provide me opportunities to see the light. He is my connection to God, who I do trust completely. I just need help realizing and living in the light.*

As demonstrated in the above entries, I still have some doubts, and I always will have them living in the world of my ego. In forgiveness, truths continue to expand, more obstacles of my ego are overcome, and I am more aware of my eternal Self. I can have more and more with less effort.

Lessons Put on My Path Expanded

BAD

Knowing that I was using the best available data for my decisions helped me early on to see that if something went wrong, it was just a mistake. This understanding was a natural progression to the *Course*'s theory that there is no sin. There are only mistakes, which can easily be forgiven. I just have to take what I learned from each mistake and move forward with no regrets. Acknowledge, and move on.

I was also able to use this with my obstacle of judgment. If I am just making mistakes, so is everyone else. I need to always remember this and offer forgiveness rather than judgment.

The Golden Rule

In forgiveness, the Golden Rule became the Platinum Rule. Instead of "Do unto others as you would have them do unto you," the Platinum Rule says "Do unto others as they would want you to do unto them,"—accept them. Do not judge anything they have done in the past or present, and be open to their future. I just want to be what others need me to be in their lives. I want to be understood, so I try to understand.

We all just want to be unconditionally loved and accepted for who we are—all of us with no exception. If I can do this for everyone I meet, I feel I am fulfilling my purpose. It's not always easy, because we cover up who we really are with our stories and drama, but the love is there. So we just need to keep trying to see it so that we can always offer our acceptance to everyone all of the time.

In guilt, I believed in karma, which says that what comes around goes around, but in grace, I found unconditional love and that there is no need for sacrifice. I still believe in cause and effect, but my new perspective is that God is the cause and that I am forever His effect.

I thought I had to give to receive, but that wasn't true, because I was always receiving God's love, no matter what I gave. I thought that was selfish in guilt, but the truth is that the more I received, the more grateful I became, and so I naturally wanted to give more. So receiving love, I became love, and I gave love.

Laughter

As mentioned earlier, the *Course* said we should have laughed at our "tiny mad idea" to separate from God, so I am glad I had laughter in my life early on. Forgiveness offers more opportunities for me to laugh and be silly—sometimes even in bad situations.

I think we all need to laugh at ourselves more often. We take our stories and ourselves way too seriously.

Nietzsche says, "Let us slay the spirit of gravity—not by wrath, but by laughter."

I also heard that a laugh is universal because it doesn't need translation and represents happiness. This is a form of the universal power I wanted. It's easy to communicate, connect with and understand everyone if we are all happy. Ella Wheeler Wilcox said, "Laugh and the world laughs with you, weep and you weep alone."

Religion to Spirituality

In grace, I learned that religion was not the path that I wanted to follow and that my real journey was spiritual. I do, however, believe that the core of every religion is love and peace, but those values get so diluted in the dogma and rules that people have applied that their true meaning is often lost.

Journal entries I recorded to note this realization are included below.

"The Miracle of Joey Ramone," by U2.
We got language so we can't communicate.
Religion so I can love and hate.
But this song also says this: "I woke up at the moment when the miracle occurred." Yay!

Reading Science of Being and Art of Living: Transcendental Meditation, *by Maharishi Mahesh Yogi. Some of the ideas I share about religion:*
It will only succeed if it brings humanity back to its source.
It should be a way to raise the consciousness of humanity to the level of God's consciousness. The purpose is to set humanity's life in tune with the laws of nature. The purpose should be to take away all of humanity's fear. It should not try to reach this purpose by creating a fear of God in the mind.

In guilt, I was focused on the Old Testament, and in grace, I found Jesus's story of love in the New Testament more valuable. In forgiveness, I learned the Bible is just another story that we use for our journeys, so it is open for interpretation. I found more evidence of love in its stories and messages. They are reflected in the below journal entries.

The Lord's Prayer

"Our Father, Who art in Heaven, hallowed be Thy name. Thy Kingdom come, Thy will be done, on earth as it is in Heaven [here and now]. Give us this day our daily bread, and forgive us our trespasses [fear and guilt] against us. Lead us not into temptation, but deliver us from evil. For Thine is the Kingdom, and the power and the glory forever and ever. Amen."

I want heaven on earth.

God doesn't bring light to us. We need to give Him darkness as our light shines. This is related to the Course as it says we need to undo the ego.

The Bible is written by man. Shouldn't be taken as concrete but as a guide. It is open to interpretation. Learned several of these interpretations through the Course and Neville.

"Father, forgive them for they know not what they do" in no way evaluates what they do. It is an appeal to God to heal their minds.

"Many are called but few are chosen" should say this: "All are called, but few have chosen to listen." Therefore, they do not choose rightly. The "chosen ones" are merely those who choose correctly sooner. Right minds can do this now, and they will find rest unto their souls. God knows us only in peace, and this is our reality.

At Chez Eugene for a mushroom omelet and some wine. I want to remember to sit here with Jesus. My image was of us just being present and able to communicate with everyone exactly as they are. We are all at peace in God's love.

Thank You for Your open heart and open arms. Take my hand, and walk with me the rest of my days here on earth and as I head toward home.

Love never gives up.
Love cares more for others than for self.
Love doesn't want what it doesn't have.
Love doesn't strut,
Doesn't have a swelled head,
Doesn't force itself on others,
Isn't always "me first,"
Doesn't fly off the handle,
Doesn't keep score of the sins of others,
Doesn't revel when others grovel,
Takes pleasure in the flowering of truth,
Puts up with anything,
Trust God always,
Never looks back,
But keeps going to the end.
—SAINT FRANCIS

---

1 Corinthians 13:1–13 says this: "Love is patient and kind. It does not envy others or brag of itself. It is not swollen with self. It is not wayward or grasping. It does not flare with anger nor harbor a grudge. It takes no joy in evil but delights in truth. It keeps all confidences, all trust, all hope, and all endurance. Love will never go out of existence. Prophesy will fail in time and languages too and knowledge as well. For we know things only partially and prophesy partially, and when the totality is known, the parts will vanish. It is like what I spoke as a child, knew as a child, thought as a child, and argued as a child—which now that I am grown up, I put aside. In the same way, we see things in a murky reflection now but shall see them full face when what I have known in part I shall know fully, just as I am known. For the present then, three things matter—believing, hoping, and loving. But supreme is loving."

Amen. God wouldn't have me be anything but love, but this was a good lesson in surrendering everything to Him, so I am open to His voice.

"He restores my soul." He doesn't reform. He restores. He doesn't camouflage the old; He restores the new.

Prodigal son. I always thought this was a lesson about doing the right thing and honoring your earthly father, but it was more about our Father's unconditional love, as He not only accepted the son back, but He also gave the son more than the son could ever imagine.

With wanting and finding more peace and love, I am becoming more open to other experiences, so I have had a couple spiritual readings. I have been amazed at some of their messages, as they evidenced, supported, or predicted my journey. Below are notes from three spiritual readings. I couldn't believe how many references appeared that spoke to things that had showed up along my journey.

Thursday, May 23, 2013
Reading with Crystal

- *Archangel Michael appeared. Protection. Looking out for me*
- *Prosperity. Don't need to worry about this. Be and know myself.*
- *Synchronicity. Listen, look for, and believe in signs. Own what I want.*

Michael, help me manifest my dreams!
- *I read Saint Michael was associated with purple and blue light. These colors have been showing up for me—also number 444.*
- *I had a dream about Michael.*

July 19, 2014
Transcript of Reading

The reader summarized what was being heard from my spiritual guides, but pointed out certain direct phrases, which are in quotes below.

Me: *Found a Course in miracles several years ago. I was so happy and couldn't stop smiling.*

Now I am content and feel more connected but not the total bliss and joy I want. What am I missing? I feel a little stuck and impatient.

I know God loves me but not sure how to feel that always here.

FORGIVENESS

Reader: *"You are loved" magnetizes. Desire to be loved. Honor yourself. "Be gentle to yourself, my child. Through your gentle heart, we may extend to you all that you have forgotten to remember."*

Me: *Feel on verge of something, spiritually and materialistically. Mostly certain but occasional doubt. My faith is strong but still have doubts.*

Moments of peace and more synchronicity, but I don't always feel on the right path.

When I look back, I see a type of guidance, but can't give up control, and I want to

Numbers come up often – 7 11 333 444 222 - multiples of 11.

Reader: *All of these feelings and happenings are reminders of "interdimensional communication."*

Me: *Health. Anxious and feeling like something's often wrong. Starting to feel confident that I am OK but still doubting. Have fears.*

Reader: *"On earth as it is in heaven." Fragmented—like you are two people. "Care of self". "Honor, and love the body that carries you. Love you through physical practice, exercise, and nutrition." You feel removed from body (outside) and this caused "decreased vitality." Become "integrated" with form. Enjoy food. Engage.*

Me: *Always have an unsettled feeling. Want to be able to just go (untethered) wherever and whenever. Travel. I often feel certain about a place (New York, Florida, or Chicago). I get settled. Then ready to move again. I don't want to work in an office anymore. The gossip and negativity weigh on me. What's next?*

Reader: *"On earth as it is in heaven." "Different." "Social service." "Focus on what you love." Peace desires "to help man move into brotherhood among men as was decreed by Jesus."*

Reader: *Jesus, "they know not what they do." I say this all of the time when someone upsets me. Michael—associated with travel and highest of all angels. "Energy moves outward. Makes things happen. Hands on." Stepping into. Being pushed "to receive." "Say yes to more."*

Need to allow universe for relationships and work.

"Compassion"—you are empathetic. Know what people need.

"You help people" They said help yourself. Will bleed through.

"Messes up." "Misstep." Need to have compassion with yourself.

Antidote for judgment—forgiveness, acceptance, and compassion.

See yourself as a little child.

"Understand that people are crying out for love."

"Honor yourself as an extension of all that is."

When you choose peace, drama will show up. When you

judge, you become part of it.

Become the eye of a hurricane. Need to become an observer. Just allow. Don't react or join in.

"Mirror"—seeing yourself more clearly and learning about yourself.

As "mirror," others may not like what they see.

"Desire to be loved." Want approval as you become more spiritual.

"On earth as it is in heaven"—deeply imprinted in record.

Reader Overview
Me: *Uploaded journals on computer. Thought about book?*

Pampered Peace Pilgrim?

Reader: *"Big charge. Embrace the unknown."*

"The gratitude that you offer is an opening to receive more and with every thank-you, comes a blessing."

"Social service." "Global." "Peace" is huge in your record. "Help others step in peace as individuals and world."

"Help humanity move into brotherhood among humans as was decreed by Jesus." "Love your brother and sister."

Will do something different.

Helping people—bring them together.

You would be a great counselor.

You like to meander.

Pampered Peace Pilgrim. Magnetism. Jump on board with not knowing how. Ask this: "I wonder how that will happen?"

I can be abundant. I won't misuse it. "That's how I am."

Cracking open the need to receive. Circle will open as you receive.

October 2015 Reading
Lizard symbol appeared. Spiritual meaning is to be set free of the limitations of the past and to be born into a higher awareness of self and abilities. The magic of lizard symbolism is extrasensory perception and clairvoyance.

"Chakras" are centers of spiritual power in the body—blue predominantly shown, which is the throat. Communication is used to soothe the soul. Seems like book is my path now.

Gratitude

Being grateful has just become so much more natural with forgiveness. I still have a gratitude journal, but I don't need to write in it as much, because being thankful is in my heart. I find myself saying thank you all the time, and the more I am grateful, more comes to me, because I know everything is being done in my best interest.

Lesson 135 of the *Course* says this: "What could you not accept, if you but knew that everything that happens, all events, past, present and to come, are gently planned by One Whose only purpose is your good? Perhaps you have misunderstood His plan, for He would never offer pain to you. But your defenses did not let you see His loving blessing shine in every step you ever took. While you made plans for death, He led you gently to eternal life."

I know this is true. There is so much evidence in my life that I can't deny this truth, and I am completely grateful!

Pampered Peace Pilgrim

I am a pampered Peace Pilgrim!!

In forgiveness, I realized I had always been a pampered Peace Pilgrim, so I chose to claim it. I knew it was what God wanted, because I felt peace. Once again, I felt my worldly journey was being used for my spiritual journey. My current pilgrimage to peace is writing this book and being God's pen while still enjoying the luxuries that are important to me—like getting a massage or having my apartment cleaned once a month. I am amazed and grateful to be able to have this project as my work. While I had a little anxiety about taking a year away from a job, I know I am being directed to do so, so that pretty much eliminates the doubt, which feels so authentic.

Peace Pilgrim quotes and my related pampered Peace Pilgrim journey follow:

"When you know your part in the scheme of things, in the Divine Plan, there is never a feeling of inadequacy. You are always given the resources for any situation, any obstacle. There is no strain; there is always security." (p.91)

"...results should never be sought or desired. Know that every right thing you do—every good word you say—every positive thought you think has good effect." (p.91)

"My desire is to strive toward perfection; to be as much in harmony with God's will as possible; to live up to the highest light I have. I am still not perfect, of course, but I grow daily. If I were perfect I would know everything and be able to do everything; I would be like God. However, I am able to do everything I am called to do, and I do know what I need to know to do my part in the Divine Plan. And I do experience the happiness of living in harmony with God's will for me." (p.126)

"All I did was to surrender my will to God's will. My entire life has prepared me for this undertaking. This is my calling. This is my vocation. This is what I must be doing. I could not be happy doing anything else." (p.127)

"Retirement should mean not a cessation of activity, but a change of activity with a more complete giving of your life to service. It should therefore be the most wonderful time of your life: the time when you are most happily and meaningfully busy." (p.160)

The Course *says -"Humility will never ask that you remain content with littleness. But it does require that you be not content with less than greatness that comes not of you." (ACIM 2007, T-18.IV.3)*

My aunt (and godmother) always remembered me on my birthday and wanted me to have nice things. I thought she was rich, and I wanted her lifestyle. Funny—she was a nun before I knew her.

Need to stop my belief in littleness. I need to believe in grandeur, because it is from God.

> *The* Course—*"You have the right to all the universe; to perfect peace, complete deliverance from all effects of sin, and to the life eternal, joyous and complete in every way, as God appointed for His holy Son. (ACIM 2007, T-25. VIII.14)*

Travel

As I mentioned in grace, I love to travel. I thought it was because I liked to visit other places, and that is true, but in forgiveness, I realized it was more about the meandering, sitting with others, and connecting with them. It also showed me that I wanted to be untethered. The physical travel in the world of my ego demonstrated my need for freedom. Once I realized this, I applied it to my overall life, which has led to a minimalist lifestyle.

In guilt and fear, I wanted stuff. I wanted to be like everyone and have what everyone had or thought I should have to feel accepted.

I shopped often and accumulated a lot of debt for things I didn't need and then worried about being in debt. I always wanted more, and I felt less important when I couldn't have what I wanted. It was a vicious cycle, and I was never really happy, because I was wasting a lot of energy buying and maintaining things.

Through grace, I started realizing I was good enough and didn't need to prove anything to others, because it was all about me and about what I thought of myself. It was at this time that I started feeling like I wanted to downsize. I was living in a three-level, furnished town house, and I decided to move to a one-bedroom apartment. I moved often after that—six times in nine years—downsizing each time. I am currently living in a small studio apartment with an efficiency kitchen, and I couldn't be happier. With each move, the only stress I had was moving the stuff, so I kept trying to get rid of anything that was not being used. This process allowed me to be able to move from Chicago to New York with everything I owned in a rented sedan. (Full disclosure though—I did have to buy a mattress upon arrival, but that is all).

It took a while to get to this point, but it was a natural progression. And I want to be clear—while I did downsize, I still like nice things and want to be pampered. You have to do what makes you happy in life. For me, I needed to get rid of stuff so that I could focus. I thought I was lazy and didn't want things to take care of, but in reality, I didn't want to be tethered, and I learned this through my journey.

Minimizing can be difficult, because I always use the justification that I might need whatever I am purging in the future. To solve this problem, I decided if I haven't used something in a while, its value is being wasted, and someone else may be able to use it. Downsizing has been so liberating and has led me to even more peace, forgiveness, and freedom from the past.

Some journal entries along the way with messages and notes that pointed to my minimalist path are included below:

When you don't have anything to lose, there is no grief, nothing to worry about, and no fear.

Becoming minimalist. Stuff really stressing me out all of the time.

In Oneness with All Life: Inspirational Selections from a New Earth, *Eckhart Tolle says, "If I am not looking to find myself in things, the attachment will drop away." Need to try this.*

I don't want a lot, but I want it to be nice and pampered. I like luxury sometimes, but I am glad I am becoming less materialistic and trying to downsize and simplify my life. I don't need a lot but just want to be comfortable with no worries about the future, which I wouldn't have if I turned everything over to God.

Tao, verse 81: living without accumulating.

I need to replace accumulating more stuff with celebrating my true essence.

The sage does not hoard,
And thereby bestows.
The more he lives for others,
The greater his life.
The more he gives to others,
The greater his abundance.

—*SAM HAMILL*

Walking here, I thought of my toes in the sand at the beach in Florida. Ready to heal there. Hope to get closer to God and put my ego away. I am getting more thoughts about abundance being my future, as I want to shed more worldly things. Probably why my stuff has been stressing me out lately. I need to see this feeling as a sign to purge more.

Peace Pilgrim quotes from *Peace Pilgrim, Her Life and Work in Her Own Words* and my related minimalist journey follow:

"She gradually and methodically adopted a life of voluntary simplicity. She began what was to be a fifteen-year period of preparation, not knowing just what it was she was preparing for." (p.xiii)

"During this 'preparation period,' she found inner peace and her calling." (p.xiii)

Me: Peace was a public speaker able to tell her truth to all that would listen. I am not a speaker, but hope my book is my outlet.

"I was trained to be generous and unselfish and at the same time trained to believe that if I wanted to be successful I must get out there and grab more than my share of this world's good. These conflicting philosophies which I had gathered from my childhood environment confused me for some time. But eventually I uprooted this false training." (p.5)

Similar for me. Very materialistic. Thought things made me happy.

"I thought it would entail a great many hardships, but I was quite wrong. Instead of hardships, I found a wonderful sense of peace and joy, and a conviction that unnecessary possessions are only unnecessary burdens." (p.12)

"There is great freedom in simplicity of living." (p.13)

"Anything that you cannot relinquish when it has outlived its usefulness possesses you." (p.19)

"We must be able to appreciate and enjoy the places where we tarry and yet pass on without anguish when we are called elsewhere. In our spiritual development we are often required to pull up roots many times and to close many chapters in our lives until we are no longer attached to any material thing and can love all people without any attachment to them." (p.19)

"To me, it was an escape from the artificiality of illusion into the richness of reality. To the world, it may seem that I had given up much. I had given up burdensome possessions, spending time meaninglessly, doing things I knew I should not do and not doing things I knew I should do. But to me, it seemed that I had gained much—even the priceless treasure of health and happiness." (p.21)

"When you become a channel through which God works there are no more limitations, because God does the work through you; you are merely the instrument—and what God can do is unlimited. When you are working for God you do not find yourself striving and straining. You find yourself calm, serene and unhurried." (p.26)

"I feel a complete protection on my pilgrimage. God is my shield. There are no accidents in the Divine Plan nor does

God leave us unattended. No one walks so safely as those who walk humbly and harmlessly with great love and great faith." (p.46)

"You know, after you have fully surrendered your life to God's will—if it is your calling to go out on faith—you will discover that even the food and shelter you need come to you very easily. Everything, even material things are given. And some amazing things are given that still surprise even me." (p.48)

"The simplification of life is one of the steps to inner peace. A persistent simplification will create an inner and outer well-being that places harmony in one's life." (p.51)

***Me** – I want to be simple but pampered!*

"Some people seem to think that my life dedicated to simplicity and service is austere and joyless, but they do not know the freedom of simplicity. I am thankful to God every moment of my life for the great riches that have been showered upon me. My life is full and good but never overcrowded. If life is overcrowded then you are doing more than is required for you to do." (p.51)

"It is those who have enough but not too much who are the happiest." (p.53)

"Because of our preoccupation with materialism we often miss the best things in life, which are free." (p.58)

"Unnecessary possessions are unnecessary burdens. If you have them, you have to take care of them." (p.58)

The simplified life is a sanctified life,

Much more calm, much less strife.
Oh, what wondrous truths are unveiled,
Projects succeed which had previously failed.
Oh, how beautiful life can be,
Beautiful simplicity. (p.58)

Transcendental Meditation

In forgiveness, Transcendental Meditation (TM) became a new tool for my spiritual path. I was introduced to this practice when I read *Super Rich: A Guide to Having It All* and *Success through Stillness*, both by Russell Simmons.

I always wanted some type of meditation in my life, so I could quiet my ego thoughts, but I could never find a type of practice that worked for me. I hear this often from others as well. For me, TM is very effective, as it doesn't say to stop thinking but to just be still and let thoughts come and go. Eventually, things will calm, and you will feel silence and freedom. I never thought I could do this twice a day for twenty minutes, but I find myself craving it more.

Another form of meditation I found is coloring. It has a similar effect of focusing on staying in the present moment. Being present is all that is needed, so you can turn any process into meditation—coloring, knitting, cleaning the house, etc. Being in the present, I see no past, and I have such a sense of peace and freedom moving forward.

Obstacles Become Blessings

In forgiveness, I knew that all of my obstacles came from fear, and for each obstacle, the fear lessened along my forgiveness journey. I will again use journal entries to demonstrate my relinquishment of fear. As I acknowledged my fears, I gave them to God. Surrender was the key.

Lack of Money

In forgiving my thoughts of lack, I know I will always have enough money to support anything that brings me peace.

Feel peaceful, happy, and content. Interacting with others without feeling distracted with guilt, worry, or fear related to other worldly things—jobs and money.

For me to feel abundant is to have enough money to get by on my own and be able to volunteer or interact with others in some way. Spiritually fulfilling—some ideas - retail, volunteering, consulting?

I have to have complete faith that God is in control of my life. I have everything I need, so I don't need to worry about anything ever.

Physical Body

I don't like to talk about health issues, because it is just part of my ego's story and creates more fear. I don't want to see myself as a body.

My fear of dying. People won't understand who I am. As ego, my fear is being misunderstood, because they don't know my real Self, so I hope my book shows them.

Nothing here matters, and only the love of God and His rules govern me. Everything comes and goes. Just move through. Shed ego and body.

Physical pain realization—if you have an ache or pain, and focus on it, it gets worse. But if you are distracted by TV, reading, or an activity, you forget about it, if just for a moment, and it's not part of your experience. This proves that being conscious of our thoughts impacts our external world – mind over body.

Cultivating your inner connection to what really matters makes the aging process less difficult.

Every material thing eventually fades away. That is nature, of which we are all a part of.

Aging well is giving yourself the freedom to be who you were meant to be.

Tao, verse 74: living with no fear of death.

I need to discontinue fearing death and remember I am not this body. I am a piece of the infinite Tao (God), never changing and never dying.

Thinking about when I die—no funeral. I want a party at Union Station's central bar (one of my favorite places). Glass of red wine for all!

"The bitterest tears shed over graves are for words left unsaid and deeds left undone," said Harriet Beecher Stowe. I think my book will say everything I want to say, so I feel blessed with this opportunity.

Lack of Self-Confidence

I shouldn't care what anyone thinks of me! I should only

care about what I think of myself. The lesson I need to learn and live!

A lesson taught to me by a Nice waiter—I can be uptight and worry about what others think, unlike the man who the waiter opened the bottle for. Or I can hope everyone accepts me like God accepts me. He is the only one I need to worry about—and not really because He loves me no matter what. How cool is that?

Holy Spirit, please help me see my grandeur and not see the ego's littleness.

I am willing to experience these things:

- *Love—true love*
- *Having more than enough money*
- *Forgetting my past and looking forward*
- *Not feeling guilty for anything*
- *Expressing my true feelings*
- *Relying on myself for my own happiness*
- *Financial freedom*

Personality Traits: Logical and Organized

In the past, I think I let my personality traits define me, which is probably why I went into finance instead of becoming a writer.

I have always been organized, logical, and methodical. It helped in my ego's career, but I thought it was boring, and I called it being anal retentive—another label added to my story.

In forgiveness, I realize its importance. As a spiritual training book, the *Course* is very logical and methodical, so I am able to grasp its lessons much more easily. I also think it has led to the natural path of minimalism. The more I want organization, the more I am willing to remove the unnecessary.

The Course *says:*

"The part of mind where reason lies was dedicated, by your will in union with your Father's, to the undoing of insanity. Here was the Holy Spirit's purpose accepted and accomplished, both at once." (ACIM 2007, T-21.V.9)

"Faith and belief, upheld by reason, cannot fail to lead to changed perception. And in this change is room made way for vision." (ACIM 2007, T-21.V.10)

"Reason is not salvation in itself, but makes way for peace and brings you to a state of mind in which salvation can be given you." (ACIM 2007, T-22.III.3)

Numbers are being used to say I'm on the right path. God is using my ego's qualities to connect me with the divine.

Middle Child

I am the middle child, and because of the gaps in our ages, my siblings and I were always at different places at different times in our lives, and we were always doing our own thing. I didn't think this was good or bad necessarily, but I think it was used to define me as part of my story.

The good that came from this is the independence that I felt as part of my path. Also, I thought I got attention by trying not to stand out, so I think I learned humility early on.

The *Course* asks me to have a different perspective of ego thoughts that don't bring me peace, and I was given the below message.

Found this article on Facebook.
Mary Ellen Klein in Wellness Feb 26, 2015

> *We've all heard the stereotypes about the successful oldest child and the laid-back youngest, but when it comes to us middle children, there aren't as many concrete generalizations out there.*
>
> *Ironically enough, the lack of thought given to labeling the middle child epitomizes the truth about us: we are often overlooked.*
>
> *It's usually not intentional, it's just that the older sibling blazes the trail for us and the younger sibling is the perpetual adorable baby, so our job is to just fit in.*
>
> *Although it can be frustrating to have to fight harder for your parents' attention, I believe there are specific benefits of being a middle child, and it's time they get pointed out:*
>
> *1. You're a peacemaker.*
>
> *You are able to see both sides of any argument and you specialize in finding the "win-win."*

> *As a kid, before bullying your younger sibling, you naturally stopped to think about how it felt when you were the victim.*
>
> *On the other hand, you also gained a better understanding of respecting your older sibling's privacy because you knew what it was like when your annoying younger sibling invaded your room.*
>
> *As a result, you are very empathetic, and you cannot choose a side in any debate without fully comprehending all perspectives involved.*
>
> *You were born for a mediating or consulting job, and people probably seek you out for advice.*
>
> *People may think you have no preference, but really you're just flexible, and you understand that the majority vote wins.*

Who knew?

As I mentioned, I love sitcoms, and I recently started watching The Middle. I knew the name came from the location of the Midwest, but for me, it's definitely more about the middle child, Sue. No matter what her external story puts against her, she is the eternal optimist to a fault, and I feel a connection to her.

The show also reflects the *Course's* theory. It starts with a conflict from some outside event; they all work internally on themselves through this event; then all is forgiven in the end. They are at peace, and as an added bonus, this is all achieved in a very funny manner!

Judgment

I saved the most difficult obstacle for last, because it has been the largest in my life and has always brought me fear and guilt. It is something I always want to try to correct, because I know forgiveness of judgment will bring me and everyone else peace.

In learning that I am creating my world, I learned about projection. What I see in others is what I see in myself. So if something or someone doesn't give me peace, I need to figure out why so that I can correct it in myself. This not only helps me improve but also makes me thankful for anything showing up in my life, knowing that they are there for a reason and to show me what I need to let go of and forgive in myself.

In forgiveness, I learned—and still believe—that I will never find God in this lifetime if I am placing any limit on Him or myself. Limits are placed when we only look at the story and judge it. This includes our own stories and for me, the things I tell myself about all of my obstacles.

Everyone is different regarding how much of their story is blocking the love in them. Some are more aware than others of how much of God's love is available to them. When Jesus was crucified, He said, "Father, forgive them for they know not what they do." This meant that they really don't know. They are so caught up in the stories of their egos that they don't see the "bad" things they do. So who are we to judge? We need to accept them, knowing that love is in them.

While judgment will always be a part of the ego's world, it is something I will always have to work on. I have always tried not to say anything bad about anyone. That doesn't mean I don't think judgy thoughts, but I can honestly say that with forgiveness, it is much less a part of my life now. I am so grateful for the peace I find in this.

Here is how judgment looks to me now:

We only see the few pages that others show us of their stories, and we only show part of our own stories. We never see the whole story, and we don't always see the love God gave us that we all share. God, however, sees the entire dream and judges us only with peace and unconditional love. It doesn't matter to Him what our stories are, because He only sees love. When we chose to see someone's entire story and the love we share with them, we are choosing God's vision, and we will see what He sees, judge as He judges, and forgive everything in everyone, including ourselves. By writing this book and sharing my fears, I feel I am showing more of my entire story, and it will be accepted. Below are entries to expound on the illustration and this idea of true forgiveness.

The Course says, "The overlooking of the battleground is now your purpose." (ACIM, T-23.IV.5)

We judge based on our stories of guilt and fear that we created, so not only should we not judge, but we also can't because we don't have all of the facts. We only have the parts of the story being projected. So the solution is to judge as the Holy Spirit would judge—only with love.

Don't make any assumptions – everyone's story is different from ours, so we shouldn't assume they want the same things we want.

See things from above the field—both sides. When we're on the field, we are defensive.

Obstacle: I don't want to be wrong and worry about what people think of me. Insecure. I want to give that to the Holy Spirit also. I know I need to stop judging others also, so I'll work on that. Feeling less judgy lately but know that changes the more I am around others, so this will be a constant need for correction.

When I let go of all of my grievances, I will know I am perfectly safe. Peace and love will surround me.

When I hold grievances, my world just gets darker and full of more clouds, but if I can forgive and let go of all my grievances, I move toward the light, God, and my true Self. I take everyone with me. I feel safe with this thought. Nothing can harm me as I move toward the light, because God is there waiting for me to be with Him again.

I've always seen things from many sides or wanted to see others from a different perspective, but when I am attacked, I forget this and judge others before looking at myself, because I don't want to be wrong. I have to remember that "above all else I want to see" and that "above all else I want to see things differently" (The Course, *lessons 27 and 28).*

Justice=just is. No right or wrong. We don't have all the information when we judge, so we need to allow the Holy Spirit to judge for us, which would be only from love and acceptance.

The Course's *Manual For Teachers, page 10: How is judgment relinquished?*

"It is necessary for the teacher of God to realize, not that he should not judge, but that he cannot." "Recognizing that judgment was always impossible for him, he no longer attempts it. This is no sacrifice. On the contrary, he puts himself in a position where judgment through him rather than by him can occur. And this judgment is neither good nor bad. It is the only judgment there is, and it is only one: God's Son is guiltless, and sin does not exist."

As noted in the above, the *Course* showed me that I need to turn all judgment over to God. His justice is all that matters, because He is the only God that can see in totality and because His judgment will always be that of love. No one is guilty of anything! We just need to trust God, look past our stories, and love everyone, including ourselves.

Jesus said, "Forgive us our trespasses as we forgive those who have trespassed against us." He understood that the first step of forgiveness is to accept other people just as they are, even if they have harmed us.

Peace Pilgrim quotes and my related judgment journey follow:

"My motives were pure and much of my work did have a positive and good effect. I used what I call spiritual therapy: I found all the good things that those I worked with wanted to do, and I helped them to do those things." (p.12)

Me – *I try to listen to everyone.*

"*My approach is to help with cause rather than effect. When I help others, it is by instilling within them the inspiration to work out problems by themselves. If you feed a man a meal, you only feed him for the day—but if you teach a man to grow food, you feed him for a lifetime.*" (p. 60)

I always used this analogy but with fishing!

What Forgiveness Looks Like Now

With overcoming obstacles, and with judgment becoming less a part of my life, new thoughts have developed. They include the thoughts below.

No Past

Lily Tomlin says, "Forgiveness means giving up all hope for a better past."

No "should have could have would have." Acknowledge, and move on! I did everything on the best available data I had at the time.

The Course *and forgiveness asks that we let the past go. If we aren't dwelling on the past, we can be in the moment with God. How many times have I been worried about something? How many of those times do I remember now? They came and went. All were resolved, so I can have faith that everything— all the problems in this world—will be resolved. This too shall pass. It is finished because we are eternal and God is always working for our best interests, so we just need to remember this through every situation and listen to Him always.*

The Course says, "*The miracle enables you to see your brother without his past, and so perceive him as born again. His errors are all past, and by perceiving him without them you are releasing him. (ACIM, T-13.VI.5)*

"*When you have learned to look on everyone with no reference at all to the past, either his or yours as perceived it, you will be able to learn from what you see now." (ACIM, T-13-VI.2)*

"*To be born again is to let the past go, and look without condemnation upon the present." (ACIM, T-13.VI.3)*

All "problems" are solved in time, because one problem had one solution. I am not separate from God. I just need to be patient, knowing that all will be OK and that anything is possible with God.

Appreciative inquiry—ask what can I do next to resolve this instead of why did this happen. Much more productive!

Insanity is doing the same thing twice and expecting different results.

Bono said, "We glorify the past when the future dries up."

I never really was a picture person. Mostly because I never thought I looked good in any picture taken of me, but I also have always wanted to look forward. I was always excited for what was next. My grandmother always told me to not wish my life away, as I was always saying, "I wish this would happen now." Ready for some event to occur to make me happy. Impatient. She was teaching me to stay in the moment at an early age. Thanks, Nanny! Now I never take pictures, because I feel it takes me out of the moment.

The Forgiveness Network 9/21, *by Tom Carpenter speaks to how scale doesn't matter with regard to forgiveness.*

"We frequently feel that if we expose in great detail how terrible things, such as the holocaust, have been, we will surely never allow them to occur again. History proves this is not the case. Holocausts, large and small, occur each time I judge myself, and my brother, as unworthy of being loved. Each time I want the stories we tell of hate and fear to be more real than risking to rely on that loving peace we share with God, there is a cutting off in my mind of one that God created brother to me. What ends the need for holocausts is remembering that I am loved and expressing that in great detail by sharing the Presence of Love within me and everyone I meet!"

No Opinion/No Complaining

Working on having no judgment and letting the past go. I find I have less opinions, and this is a good thing. I think they can be hurtful, because they create defensiveness rather than acceptance. All of our stories are different, so what is right for one may not be for another, and that's OK. An opinion doesn't matter.

Just realized that something I always do is change my opinions as more information becomes available. I also see or try to see everything from the other side or how it may have a different meaning. Need to give myself more credit for not being so judgy.

"Nothing is more conducive to peace of mind than not having an opinion," says Lichtenberg. It is what it is. My opinion doesn't change anything. Saying "whatevs" creates peace. Cable news is exhausting. No facts anymore—just opinion.

How amazing would it be if we used all of the energy from arguing our opinion to actually solving the problem?

Words hurt, so we really need to be careful what we say to each other and remember how we would feel if we heard something derogatory about ourselves. "put yourself in the other person's shoes." I really don't like the word "stupid." I cringe every time I hear it. I truly believe there is no such thing as a stupid question—forgiveness proves no one is stupid. They just don't know any better at the time, and we all need to understand that about each other and the circumstances that occur in our lives.

Also don't like the word "hate." Such a strong word and judgment of a situation, especially for things we don't know everything about.

Tao, Verse 49: Living Beyond Judgment says:
I need to see myself as flexible, since being open is the highest virtue. I can pride myself by extending my goodness and kindness to all sides, even when they oppose my thinking.

I should avoid taking one position and sticking to it no matter what the circumstances are and should be in harmony with all people, especially those whose opinions conflict with mine. I also need to remember to include myself when giving kindness and not judging.

Affirm—I see myself in this person, and I choose to be in a space of goodness rather than judgment.

A commercial said this: "See me, don't stare at me."

"Namaste" means "I honor the place in you where we are all one."

I need to become a "noticer," decreasing my criticism while increasing the amount of courtesy and goodness in the world.

Opinions are ineffective—always believed if you're not part of the solution, you're part of the problem. Working in office environment or with public, there is a lot of opinions and complaining rather than trying to offer solutions. Another reason I don't want to work in an office any longer.

I always try to never complain. It adds more drama and negative energy to a situation that I can't control and solves nothing.

I can sometimes be impatient—that has lessened with having no opinion and with not complaining about the situations I am in—they are what they are.

Complaining—what good does it do? Absolutely nothing! Enough said!

Chapter 7

Not a Conclusion – What's Next?

Below are journal entries in forgiveness that demonstrate my current path, feelings of divine connection, prayers, how blessed I feel now and what's next.

Synchronicity lately. Images, déjà vu, numbers—all appearing more and more in my life. Feeling guided.

"God, please use me." "Direct my steps"

Want to work on book now that it's getting cold in Chicago. Holy Spirit, help me to continue to try to find my connection to God's mind. Help me just always keep talking to You, be open to God's love, and remember Jesus's Resurrection and the feelings of certainty, freedom, peace, calm, and stillness. Freedom from my past. Oneness with all life.

I am excited about the future. So many happy thoughts about going back to New York. Getting rid of more stuff. Not working. Knowing more and more all will be OK. Feeling guided. Letting fears go. Being healthier. Thinking less about the past. (Letting things go more and more and quicker.) Happy thoughts more present. Feeling more creative. Book seems to be flowing. Pampered Peace Pilgrim more my reality as I become more real.

FORGIVENESS

Forgiveness—seeing everyone as if for the first time. No story. No drama. Accepting of who they are. This can be easy with strangers, but difficult with those we are close to or have to deal with often, because of our histories. Have to do this for ourselves. Let go of guilt, fear, and the past.

Start from now. Certain all will be OK. Don't take the past into the future, knowing God is guiding me. Freedom —home, peace, and heaven on earth.

New travel wish list:
- *The Camino*
- *Paris*
- *Dublin*
- *Nature spas—nature without the bugs*

God, show me how! I am ready!

Remembering Ray from a project with New York Cares that I did several years ago. I loved helping him with his homework after school, and I want to do more volunteer work, especially with kids. They make my spirit smile.

Where is your ego getting in the way? Make the connection to your true Self so that you don't have to operate from ego. Be aware. Look for peace. When we get upset, we need to say this: "That must be my ego."

"It is finished." The dream is done, and I just need to follow God's way so that I can go home—awake.

Course *Lesson 200: "There is no peace except the peace of God."*

> *"Peace is the bridge that everyone will cross to leave this world behind."*
>
> *"Peace is the answer to conflicting goals, to senseless journeys, frantic, vain pursuits, and meaningless endeavors [story/drama]. Now the way is easy and is sloping gently toward the bridge where freedom lies within the peace of God."*
>
> *"Let us not lose our way again today. We go to heaven, and the path is straight. Only if we attempt to wander can there be delay and needless wasted time on thorny ways. God alone is sure, and He will guide our footsteps. He will not desert His Son in need nor let Him stray forever from His home. The Father calls; the Son will hear."*

By forgiving, I am starting over and giving everyone, including myself, a new beginning to be accepted. I am bringing peace to every situation—that is happiness and freedom.

I have shared my journey, which includes many lessons I believe God gave me to pass along as His pen—from guilt (fear) through grace (love) to our goal of peace (forgiveness).

I hope I have provided a spiritual guidebook for everyone to share with others so that their journeys are enhanced and so that they find the peace I have found.

I am grateful to everyone on my path who allowed me to undo my story through this book. This line from the Ten Commandments comes to mind: "So let it be written, so let it be done." Jesus's words on the cross also come to mind: "It is finished." My guilt story is over, and with grace, I continue my journey of peace for everyone and myself.

I decided that after my book was published, I would burn my journals that contributed to the story so far. I feel that this journey is complete, that this part of the story is undone, and that I am more untethered and ready for more freedom. I will open a new journal, ask God "what's next?" and give Him the pen once again to continue my path on peace.

More to Share

In guilt and grace, messages were subtle, but in forgiveness, they became more obvious and presented themselves more frequently through my favorite pastimes of books, theater shows, movies, and songs. From each, I would always write down whatever thoughts would resonate in my soul. I would like to share some of these thoughts as my pen to be used, as desired, for your story. While some of the messages below seem to be repeated, they are said in different words, and I think this is helpful because some truths need repeating. I am only providing samples of each source, but all are worthy of experiencing in their entirety.

Books

The Seven Spiritual Laws of Success: A Practical Guide to the Fulfillment of Your Dreams, by Deepak Chopra

Advice is provided within each of the seven laws, so I try to apply this advice whenever I remember.

Pure Potentiality

Practice not judging.

Giving

I need to commit to keeping the wealth circulating in my life by giving and receiving gifts of peace, caring, affection, appreciation, and love.

Karma and Cause and Effect

Witness the choices I make in each moment.

Whenever I make a choice, ask these questions: "What are the consequences of this choice? Will this choice bring fulfillment and happiness to me and also to those who are affected by this choice?"

Least Effort

Accept people, situations, circumstances, and events as they occur.

This means taking responsibility by not blaming anyone or anything for my situation. Know that every problem is an opportunity to ask for help from God and that He will answer, so no worry or effort is needed.

Don't be defensive. Give up my need to defend my point of view. Remain open to all points of view. No opinion!

Intention and Desire

Give up your attachment to outcome, and focus on intention. What brings me peace?

Let the universe handle the details.

Detachment

Commit to detachment. Allow myself and those around me the freedom to be as they are.

Factor in uncertainty as an essential ingredient of my experience.

Get excited about all that can occur when I remain open to the infinity of choices.

Dharma and Purpose in Life

Seek my higher Self. Awaken myself to the deep stillness within me.

Ask this: "How can I serve?"

Dialogue on Awakening, **by Tom Carpenter**

My Course mentor introduced me to Tom Carpenter. He has a way of expressing the theory of the Course for anyone to understand.

"You do not trust yourself because you have taught yourself to rely on the judgment of others as being the standard of your worth." (p.14)

"Attempting to change yourself instead of accepting yourself gives your ego another path to pursue and will only perpetuate that entire process. It will also perpetuate unhappiness and disappointment." (p.60)

"A more helpful focus for your attention is simply that it is a dream. And by a dream, I mean it is a sense of yourself that is not real. In the sense that you have made a physical

backdrop as the stage upon which to perform your comedy/ drama, knowing that the part you are playing is but a caricature of your Self, do think of it as a playground. And with this recognition, play your part joyfully." (p.82)

"Think of it, if you will, as a process of bringing yourself out of a state of amnesia." (p.85)

"Letting go of your intellectual curiosity and allowing yourself to relax into the trust of your feelings of Love are what will eventually allow you to communicate on the truest level possible throughout the universe, wherever you direct your attention with that Loving feeling." (p.112)

"It will not be in the past that you will find reasons to forgive yourself. It is in the presence of your current awareness that you know your Self to be guiltless. It is here and now that you feel resonance when I suggest that you are the divinely perfect Creation of God." (p.169)

Change Your Thoughts and Change Your Life: Living the Wisdom of the Tao, by Wayne Dyer

The Tao is an excellent path to follow for a divine life, and Wayne Dyer does an excellent job of explaining how each verse applies to our everyday life. I am only providing the 81 verses. I highly recommend this source for anyone interested in the Tao and a natural path.

Living...

1 The Mystery, 2 The Paradoxical Unity, 3 Contentment, 4 Infinitely, 5 Impartially, 6 Creatively, 7

Beyond Ego, 8 In the Flow, 9 Humility, 10 Oneness, 11 From the Void, 12 With Inner Conviction, 13 With an Independent Mind, 14 Beyond Form, 15 An Unhurried Life, 16 With Constancy, 17 As an Enlightened Leader, 18 Without Rules, 19 Without Attachment, 20 Without Striving, 21 The Elusive Paradox, 22 With Flexibility, 23 Naturally, 24 Without Excess, 25 From Greatness, 26 Calmly, 27 By Your Inner Light, 28 Virtuously, 29 By Natural Law, 30 Without Force, 31 Without Weapons, 32 The Perfect Goodness of the Tao, 33 Self-Mastery, 34 The Great Way, 35 Beyond Worldly Pleasures, 36 In Obscurity, 37 In Simplicity, 38 Within Your Own Nature, 39 Wholeness, 40 By Returning and Yielding, 41 Beyond Appearances, 42 By Melting into Harmony, 43 Softly, 44 By Knowing When to Stop, 45 Beyond Superficialities, 46 Peacefully, 47 By Being, 48 By Decreasing, 49 Beyond Judgment, 50 As an Immortal, 51 By Hidden Virtue, 52 By Returning to the Mother, 53 Honorably, 54 As if Your Life Makes a Difference, 55 By Letting Go, 56 By Silent Knowing, 57 Without Authoritarianism, 58 Untroubled by God or Bad Fortune, 59 By Thrift and Moderation, 60 With Immunity to Evil, 61 By Remaining Low, 62 In the Treasure House of the Tao, 63 Without Difficulties, 64 By Being Here Now, 65 By Staying Simple-Hearted, 66 By Emulating the Sea, 67 By the Three Treasures, 68 By Cooperation, 69 Without Enemies, 70 A God-Realized

Life, 71 Without Sickness, 72 With Awe and Acceptance, 73 In Heaven's Net, 74 With No Fear of Death, 75 By Demanding Little, 76 By Bending, 77 By Offering the Surplus, 78 Like Water, 79 With out Resentments, 80 Your Own Utopia, 81 Without Accumulating

Three Magic Words, by Uell S. Andersen

Through reading Wayne Dyer, this book was introduced to me. I won't make you wait to find out what the "Three Magic Words" are. They are "I AM GOD," which sounded arrogant to me, like the title of my book, but I get it now and hope the reader does as well. This book provides more support for the *Course's* premise that God has never left us. It is also a source of excellent meditations.

"Yet inside you, a still small voice knows the truth, and no matter the strength of your rebellion away from your true self, the fact of your spiritual existence, the great I AM, will not be denied." (p.16)

"There is a power far greater than you and which you can use to make your life happy and fulfilled. The understanding of the power within yourself will expand your life to new and exciting horizons, will embark you upon the greatest adventure it is possible to know." (p.16)

"God did not create the evil; He simply endowed you with the prime function to create, and He allowed you to create what you will." (p.28)

"I accept good, and the supply and love of the universe are mine." (p.47)

"Know that your every step is unerringly guided on a perfect route to your destination." (p.123)

"Whatever has developed in our experience has not been brought to us by luck or fate or coincidence, but is simply a physical manifestation of our thought and belief." (p.142)

"The moment we say something is impossible, we make it impossible for God to manifest it through us." (p.210)

Reading books from Wayne Dyer also led me to Neville Goddard, who was a huge influence in connecting my Christian background with the *Course*. I also think it's interesting that before I found his works, I had a Siamese cat—the love of my life—named Neville. My kitty got his name from a cute Fig Newton commercial that always made me smile.

Your Faith Is Your Fortune, **by Neville Goddard**

"You are constantly drawing to yourself that which you are conscious of being. Change your conception of yourself from that of the slave to that of Christ." (p.15)

"Now you will realize why Jesus sanctified Himself instead of others, why to the pure all things are pure, why in Christ Jesus (the awakened consciousness) there is no condemnation. Awake from the sleep of condemnation and prove the principle of life. Stop not only your judgment of others but your condemnation of yourself." (p.25)

"Far from being a day of mourning, Good Friday should be a day of rejoicing for there can be no resurrection or expression unless there is first a crucifixion or impression. The thing to be resurrected in your case is that which you desire to be. You must feel that 'I AM the resurrection and the life of the desire.'" (p.40)

"Every problem automatically produces the desire of solution." (p.43)

"When you can look upon man as one grand brotherhood without distinction of race or creed, then you will know that you have severed adhesions. With these ties cut, all that now separates you from your true being is your belief that you are man." (p.45)

"So create a new heaven, enter into a new state of consciousness and a new earth will appear." (p.63)

"Man discovers his awareness of being to be the inexhaustible treasure of the universe. In that day when man makes this discovery he dies as man and awakes as God." (p.71)

Awakened Imagination, by Neville Goddard

"Through imagination we disarm and transform the violence of the world." (p.3)

"The Son of God is not to be found in history nor in any external form. He can only be found as the imagination of him in whom His presence becomes manifest." (p.5)

"We must go on imagining better than the best we know." (p.5)

"'Father forgive them' is not the plea that comes once a year but the opportunity that comes every day." (p.37)

"To consciously create circumstances, man must consciously direct his inner speech, matching 'the still small voice' to his fulfilled desires." (p.53)

"Be more interested in what you are inwardly saying now than what you have 'said' by choosing wisely what you think and what you feel now." (p.55)

"Any time we feel misunderstood, misused, neglected, suspicious, afraid, we are spending our thoughts and wasting our time. Whenever we assume the feeling of being what we want to be, we are investing." (p.55)

"We cannot abandon the moment to negative inner talking and expect to retain command of life." (p.55)

The Pilgrimage, **by Paulo Coelho**

This work, and his most popular book, *The Alchemist*, should be read by anyone wanting to understand the journey.

"When you travel, you experience, in a very practical way, the act of rebirth. You confront completely new situations, the day passes more slowly, and on most journeys you don't even understand the language the people speak. So you are like a child just out of the womb." (p.35)

"And most important, that you have to find support for yourself in the love that consumes during every minute of the climb, because it is that love which directs and justifies your every step." (p.163)

"And only when that happens—when you accept your role as a Master—will you learn all the answers you have in your heart." (p.222)

"All at once, I felt exhausted by all that time spent on tests and battles and lessons and the pilgrimage." (p.256)

"This was a cross that I need not set upright, for it was there before me, solitary and immense, resisting time and the elements. It was a symbol of the fate that people created, not for their God but for themselves." (p.256)

"It is not a sin to be happy." (p.257)

"He said that I should forget forever my unworthiness because the power had been reborn in me, in the same way that it could be reborn in all people who devote their lives to the good fight. A day would come—said the lamb's eye—when people would once again take pride in themselves, and then all of nature would praise the awakening of the God that had been sleeping within them." (p.259)

The Untethered Soul, **by Mark Singer**

"Do not let anything that happens in life be important enough that you're willing to close your heart over it." (p.46)

"If you close and protect yourself, you are locking this scared, insecure person within your heart. You will never be free that way." (p.61)

"Because you got rid of that scared part of you, you don't ever have to worry about getting hurt or disturbed. You no longer have to listen to 'What will they think of me?' or, 'Oh God, I wish I hadn't said that. It sounded so stupid.' You just

go about your business and put your whole being into whatever's happening, instead of putting your whole being into your personal sensitivity." (p.62)

"Fear is the cause of every problem." (p.73)

"The purpose of spiritual evolution is to remove the blockages that cause your fear." (p.73)

"It is actually possible to never have another problem for the rest of your life. This is because events are not problems; they're just events. Your resistance to them is what causes the problem. But, again, don't think that because you accept reality it means you don't deal with things. You do deal with them. You just deal with them as events that are taking place on the planet Earth, and not as personal problems." (p.153)

"There is no reason to be afraid of life. And the fear will fade once you understand that the only thing there is to get from life is the growth that comes from experiencing it." (p.161)

Theater Shows

When I lived in New York, I loved the theater and saw many shows. I would always enjoy the theater for the entertainment, costumes, dance, and music, but then messages started to present themselves. So after each show, I would write down the theme, song, or idea that related to forgiveness, guidance for my journey, or concepts to share.

Catch Me if You Can
At the end says good-bye to old ways and wants a home where he is loved—like our home with God.

Rent: Seasons of Love
That's how we should measure. "Measure in love." Life is about choosing love over fear. We only have this moment.

The Mountaintop
MLK's final days. Getting over fear to return home. The angel used laughter. Reminded me of the Course. And choose God when we had the tiny mad idea to separate from God.

Godspell
An easier way for me to get Jesus's messages through songs and humor.

"Prepare Ye…the Way of the Lord."

"Day by Day"

Oh sweet Lord, three things I pray:

To know Thee more clearly,

Love Thee more dearly,

Follow Thee more nearly.

"You cannot serve two masters, God and Money [ego]."

Lead in Godspell, Hunter Parrish, had Matthew 7:13 in bio: "Enter through the narrow gate. For wide is the gate and broad is the road that leads to destruction, and many enter through it."

Porgy and Bess
All about faith and God. Porgy was a beggar who had "plenty of nothing," but he was happy and trusted in God.

Death of a Salesman
Many Course lessons. "My salvation came from taking interest in nothing." Last line: "We're free."

Evita
Said it was an illusion—the world she created.

Priscilla
Accept everyone always. "True Colors" was a powerful song.
   God speaking: "But I see your true colors shining through and that's why I love you. So don't be afraid to let them show. Your true colors, true colors are beautiful, like a rainbow."

Ghost
Right here right now. Need to stay in the moment with God. No past and the present extends for all of us into a certain future with our Father. We are already OK.

A Christmas Carol
Scrooge says, "We don't know anything."

Charlotte's Web
Terrific. Radiant. Humble.
   Lost blue ribbon. Then accepted things and was given

more than could be imagined! (Prodigal Son) Help me surrender all to You!

An American Idiot
At the U2 concert in Hawaii, the band played with Green Day. I was only a little familiar with their music at the time. When I arrived in New York, they had turned their album, *American Idiot*, into a Broadway show, and it was a punk rock version of *A Course in Miracles* for me. I lost count of how many times I saw it, and I am sure my friends thought I was crazy.

If you were a fan of the album or Broadway show, they could be enjoyed for the songs alone, but they had such a profound message for me since they symbolized the *Course's* message.

This hero's journey is of three post-9/11 guys from California that are not happy with the world they have now come to know. They are bitter and resentful. They try to fix their stories, but in the end, they only want to go home.

I don't know if Billy Joe Armstrong read *A Course in Miracles*, but the lyrics in his songs seemed to relay its message perfectly.

Here is the story and the *Course's* translation of the lyrics:

It starts with the song "American Idiot," which states that "all across the alienation, everything isn't meant to be OK." In our egos' stories, we'll always be searching for home externally and not satisfied here.

The character Jesus of Suburbia is introduced and says there is nothing wrong with him, because this is how he is supposed to be in "the land of make believe."

In the next several songs, the lyrics demonstrate our unconsciousness and how we repeat our mistakes and live externally until we hear the call to come home and live more consciously.

"City of the Damned"
At the end of another lost highway,
Signs misleading to nowhere.

"Tales from Another Broken Home"
I lost my faith to this, this town that don't exist.
Running away from pain when you've been victimized.

"Holiday"
I beg to dream and differ from the hollow lies.
Trials by fire setting fire
Is not a way that's meant for me.

Course – *We feel confused at this time—there is a duality as we live our ego's life and seek our spiritual path.*

"Boulevard of Broken Dreams"
I am walking down the line
That divides me somewhere in my mind

"Are We the Waiting?"
Forget-me-nots and second thoughts live in isolation.
The rage and love, the story of my life.

"Wake Me Up When September Ends"
As my memory rests,
But never forgets what I lost.
Wake me up when September ends

"Homecoming"
I am standing all alone.
Please call me only if you are coming home.

"East 12th Street"
So far away. I don't want to stay.
I just want to be free.
This life-like dream ain't for me.

"We're Coming Home Again"
Underneath their feet, the time has come
And it's going nowhere.
We're the ones going home.

"Good Riddance"
So make the best of this test, and don't ask why.
It's not a question, but a lesson learned in time.

Movies

Movies played a big role in my life also. I love the entire experience. Sitting in a theater with popcorn, diet coke, and candy. An escape from reality for a while.

Like the theater, it all started as entertainment, but then I started paying attention to the messages that were meant to appear as part of my journey. I usually watched light and airy romantic comedies, but I started going outside my box so that I could get more of these types of messages. If you like movies, I recommend all of these, if you're looking for some of the insight I received. The overall message of any movie is that anything is possible, and an Oreo Mini commercial that I saw at a movie spoke to this. It's what's deep inside that's wonder filled.

Wonder if we tried a new thing
Looked inside, see what we can bring
Forget who you're supposed to be,
Take all your crazy flavors, show them all to me
If we dare to wonder about what holds us down,
The fears, the doubts,
Could we spark something, watch it grow?
Be more wonder filled than we know.

Some movies where I felt God's presence because they shared a message related to my journey are listed below.

Field of Dreams
Probably my favorite movie of all time. "If you build it, they will come." The "field" for me is my book. I hope if I write it, they will read it.

Hugo
One of the most emotional movies I've ever watched. I didn't know why at the time, but after some thought, I figured out the key line "If you lose your purpose, it's like you're broken" was absolutely speaking to my inner Self.

It demonstrated the platinum rule when the boy cried out to the world: "You should understand."

He received a secret message from his father that led him home.

From a broken robot? I thought it was broken but learned from the grandfather that it and he weren't broken – none of us are.

"If we don't know our purpose, we become sad."

At the end, Hugo asked to be heard. He didn't know why, but he needed someone to listen. I cried so much!

The Wizard of Oz
You've always had the power. It's God's love and my real Self!

Under the Tuscan Sun
Anything is possible. So take a leap of faith.

The Beautiful Exotic Marigold Hotel
"It will all be all right in the end, so if it's not all right, then

it's not the end." My end is remembering God.

Second Best Exotic Marigold Hotel
"No Death. Just let go of the story."

The Martian
Solve one problem (and there is only one) at a time and then go home.

Invictus
Movie and poem about humility and forgiveness at work in one person. I have to look within and make the choice for God. "I am the master of my fate. I am the captain of my soul."

Toy Story 3
We all just want to be loved.

Avatar
Everyone wants to be heard. When they met each other, they said, "I see you," and meant their higher and inner Self.

Inception
About turning over guilt to wake up to the real world.

The Help
I laughed and cried. Message at the end—"Live your truth, and you will be free!"

The Smurfs
(Yes, The Smurfs.) About living what matters. Had a moment when I didn't have a worry. Knew all would be OK.

Idiot Brother
Give people the benefit of the doubt, and they will rise to the occasion. I want this perspective—acceptance and love of all.

Moneyball
The last line of song is this: "Just enjoy the show." Another message was that it all came down to the last game. Nothing else really mattered—like our dream here. All that matters is returning home—not how we get there.

The Way
A journey on the Camino de Santiago de Compostela (the Camino). I would love to do this.

Megamind
About being two people—good and evil. He decided to be good. It's a choice.

New Year's Eve
Message about having faith and hope and showing forgiveness.

We Bought a Zoo
It was very good and helped me focus on putting my faith in God for my future. All will work out according to God's plan.

The Lorax
I am the "seed."

"Unless someone like you cares a whole awful lot, nothing is going to get better. It's not."

Salmon Fishing in the Yemen
Had moments when I realized the message of possibilities and felt anything is possible for my life because of God.

The Perks of Being a Wallflower
"We accept the love that we think we deserve. I feel infinite."

Rise of the Guardians
Jack Frost's center was "fun." I asked this: "What is my center?" Then I thought this: "God and forgiveness." Wanted to use my center to be a guardian and teacher for the world.

Life of Pi
(Tom, this is for you.) Good. Visual. A lot of symbolism that may take me a while to figure out.

Pi is the tiger. Spent the entire time trying to help it survive, tame it, and live with it. Then it just left without saying good-bye, so he wept. Is the tiger the ego? Surrenders to God and at that point lives with the tiger.

Oz: The Great and Powerful
Taught about faith and not living by fear. Many messages to help guide my path these days.

The Croods
They lived in darkness. Motto is this: "Never not be afraid." Until they found the light and freedom.

Smurfs 2 *(If you see Smurfs 1, you have to see Smurfs 2)*
It doesn't matter what you are. It's who you chose to be.

The Painting
Lola, an unfinished character in a painting, was looking for the artist (God). She knew He was there and had faith and found Him.

The subjects were able to complete themselves. God had given them all they needed. Lola was happy with herself and accepted everyone.

Songs

The Course says this: "Listen, and see if you remember an ancient song you knew so long ago and held more dear than any melody you taught yourself to cherish since." (ACIM 2007, T-21.I.7)

Music is another form of God's pen, and lines from the songs below stuck in my head. They would always come to mind often, and they spoke to me enough to write down in my journal.

When I was young, my sister had the Eagles' greatest-hits album, and I loved the song "Take It Easy."

The first line always pops into my head: "I'm just running down the road trying to loosen my load."

My "load" is my story, and I am sure this has driven me to my minimalist ways. Also, when I started learning about chakras, the seven centers of spiritual power in the human body, I thought of a funny new version of the song for my journey.

"Take It Easy"
I am just meandering down the road,
Trying to loosen my load.
I've got seven chakras on my mind.

One, he wants to ground me.
Four, they want to balance me.
Two, put love in my heart.

Take it easy.
Take it easy.

Don't let the sound of my own voice and ego drive me crazy,
Lighten up while I still can.
Don't even try to understand.

"Que Sera Sera"
Whatever will be, will be

"Imagine" – John Lennon – another Peace Pilgrim
Imagine all the people

Living life in peace

You may say I am a dreamer
But I am not the only one

And the world will be as one.

"Free Your Mind" – *En Vogue*
Free your mind and
The rest will follow.

"Take It All" – *Third Day*
Take it all, cause I can't take it any longer
All I have, I can't make it on my own.

Here I am, all I have
Take it all!

U2

I have mentioned Bono's influence on my journey. Below are just a few lines from certain U2 songs to give you an idea of the message I heard along my journey. I would recommend you listen to them in their entirety to get all you can out of them.

"Sunday Bloody Sunday"
The real battle just begun.
To claim the victory Jesus won

"I Still Haven't Found What I'm Looking For"

You broke the bonds
You loosed the chains

You carried the cross
And my shame

For me, this was one of the most influential songs. It was saying that as egotistical people, we will never be satisfied here, but we know happiness is possible because of Jesus.

Another line in the song says this: "I have spoken with the tongue of angels." This comes from 1 Corinthians 13:1, which says, "If I speak in the tongues of men and of angels, but have not love, I am only a resounding gong or a clanging cymbal." Love is the goal!

Rattle and Hum

This is probably my favorite album. The lyrics tell us to look within, follow Jesus, and find love.

In the song "All Along the Watchtower," the line "All I've got is a red guitar, three chords and the truth" reminded me of the Holy Trinity. They were my three chords leading me to the truth.

"Silver and Gold"

(Could be referring to materialism but demonstrates need to look internally to be free.)

These chains no longer bind me
Nor the shackles at my feet
Outside are the prisoners
Inside the free

"Love Rescue Me"
Beautifully explains our journey. Cries for love to rescue us. The cry is heard, and freedom is found.

I've conquered my past
The future is here at last

"When Love Comes to Town"
Once we know love and Jesus, there's no turning back. What we've done in the past doesn't matter, because we always have God's love.

I was there when they crucified my Lord.
But I've seen love conquer the great divide.

"God Part II"
Like I am spinning on a wheel
It always stops beside a name
A presence I can feel
I, I believe in love

"All I Want Is You"
All the promises we make

From the cradle to the grave
When all I want is you

Achtung Baby

"One" We Are All United in God
"We get to carry each other."

"All That You Can't Leave Behind"
About leaving and leaving behind. It addresses questions we need to ask along our journey. What do we take along, and what can last?

"Beautiful Day"
Touch me, take me to that other place
Teach me, I know I am not a hopeless case

"Elevation"
I've lost all self-control
Been living like a mole

You make me feel like I can fly
So high, elevation

"Walk On"
And love is not the easy thing
The only baggage you can bring
Is all that you can't leave behind

"Grace"

Because grace makes beauty
Out of ugly things

How to Dismantle an Atomic Bomb

"All Because of You"

Everything was ugly but your beautiful face
And it left me no illusion

All because of you
I am…I am

References

A Course in Miracles Combined Volume Third Edition. Mill Valley: Foundation for Inner Peace, 2007.

Peace Pilgrim: Her Life and Work in Her Own Words. Santa Fe, New Mexico: Friends of Peace Pilgrim, 1991.

Anderson, Uell. *Three Magic Words*. First Paperback Edition. USA: Create Space Independent Publishing Platform, 2011.

Carpenter, Tom. *Dialogue on Awakening, Communion with a Loving Brother*. Linda and Tom Carpenter, 2012.

Chopra, Deepak. *The Seven Spiritual Laws of Success, A Practical Guide to the Fulfillment of Your Dreams*. Novato, CA: New World Library, 1992.

Coelho, Paulo. *The Pilgrimage*. New York, New York: HarperCollins Publishers, 1995.

Dyer, Wayne. *Change Your Thoughts and Change Your Life: Living the Wisdom of the Tao*. New York, New York: Hay House, Inc., 2007.

Goddard, Neville. *Your Faith Is Your Fortune*. Blacksburg, Virginia: Wilder Publications, 2011.

Goddard, Neville. *Awakened Imagination*. Camarillo, California: DeVorss Publications, 2010.

Singer, Michael. *The Untethered Soul: The Journey Beyond Yourself*. Oakland, California: New Harbinger Publications and Noetic Books, 2007.

Williamson, Marianne. *The Law of Divine Compensation: On Work, Money, and Miracles*. New York, New York: HarperCollins Publishers, 2012.

About the Author

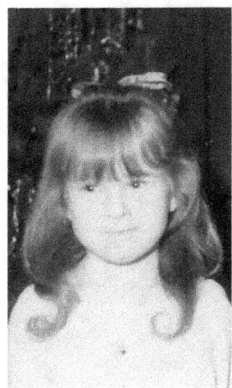 

*Left: My young self. **Right:** Me and a dog named Bo, who I met on a Seine cruise in Paris.*

Jennifer Hoerl has a Business Management degree from University of Maryland University College. She has held several finance positions, including CFO of a credit union and Finance Director for ONE, an international advocacy group working to end extreme poverty.

Now – A Writer and Pampered Peace Pilgrim!

www.ingramcontent.com/pod-product-compliance
Lightning Source LLC
Chambersburg PA
CBHW050536300426
44113CB00012B/2123